Written by Ian Souter

For Jessie and Michael
with love

Published by Scholastic Publications Ltd,
Villiers House, Clarendon Avenue,
Leamington Spa, Warwickshire CV32 5PR

© 1993 Scholastic Publications Ltd

Written by Ian Souter
Edited by Juliet Gladston
Sub-edited by Jane Wright
Illustrated by Roger Wade Walker
(Pages 116 and 117 by Roland Smith)
Front and back covers designed by Keith
Martin
Photograph by Bob Saunders, John Wright
Photography
Typeset by Typesetters (Birmingham) Ltd
Printed in England by Clays Ltd, St Ives plc
Artwork by Steve Williams Design, Leicester

**British Library Cataloguing in Publication
Data**
A catalogue record for this book is available from the
British Library.

ISBN 0-590-53085-2

Contents

74   TOPICAL POETRY

112   REPRODUCIBLE MATERIAL

125   RESOURCES

Introduction

Metaphor

Morning is
a new sheet of paper
for you to write on.

Whatever you want to say,
all day,
until night
folds it up and flies away.

The bright words and
the dark words
are gone until dawn
and a new day
to write on.

Eve Merriam

The above poem has the ability to inspire — to make you feel that each day, each new idea, each fresh piece of paper just might turn into something special. Inside its sculptured form and patterned words there lies a certain magic that can spark our imagination and fire enjoyment within us all.

Poetry, if allowed into our lives, has much to say and an important role to play. It deals with commonly shared experiences that are heightened and enriched through its particular style and usage of words, patterns and rhymes. Poetry has a quality that will stir pleasure and excite or amuse those who walk its literary paths. It is a response to a need to capture emotions and observations in a more intensified, brief and resonant form than prose.

If poetry is presented in a positive, entertaining fashion then it will be loved and enjoyed by children. However, they need time and opportunities to enjoy the rhymes and rhythms, delight in the nonsense, laugh at the mischievous imagery, absorb the thoughtful and reflect on the emotional. In our schools, the problem has been that good poetry teaching has been

far too spasmodic, although of late the resources available have certainly made it more attractive, accessible and enjoyable. Poetry in the past has, at times, been seen as an esoteric subject. A clandestine stranger that stalked the literary heights and spoke to the chosen few. It has been allowed to creep by children, in some cases virtually unseen. As educators, we have a responsibility to surround young children with the pleasure of poetry so that it appears to them to be as normal as prose. Hopefully this book will play some part in achieving this.

WHY POETRY?

Poetry is with us from our earliest years. A child sharing a nursery rhyme and interacting with a parent, a teacher or a peer is sharing in a variety of language and emotional and social skills. She is being offered an enjoyment of poetry as the sounds and the feel of the words wrap themselves rhythmically round her lips and tongue.

Poems also appeal because they come in so many different shapes and sizes; being exciting, funny, thoughtful and, at times, challenging. They can open up a whole new world of word-play for children and therefore play an important role in a child's development — affecting their sense of freedom and adventure with language. Poetry allows children to write about their surrounding world, but most importantly about themselves. If, through poetry, we can develop creative thinking and allow for fantasy and self-expression, we are surely some way to producing sensitive and thoughtful writers of the future.

HOW DO I START?

The following is a checklist of ideas that should help poetry begin to play an important and successful role in the classroom.

The teacher

● If you haven't already found the pleasure in poetry then start looking! There's plenty of it out there. Visit bookshops and libraries and find some of the titles recommended at the back of this book.
● Build up a collection of books and poems that *you* enjoy.
● Try to index by subject the poems you find the most successful. This will save a lot of time when trying to remember that elusive poem! A small file box with alphabetical cards is ideal.
● Persuade your headteacher to spend some money on poetry resources. However, you may have to be prepared to dig into your own pocket — in the long run it will be well worth it.
● Scan the back issues of magazines like *Child Education* and *Junior Education* for interesting articles on poetry.

● Read reviews on poetry books, then find out if your local bookshop has a copy that you can look at. It may save you wasting money buying a book which is of little use to you.
● Look out for in-service courses at your local teachers' centre.
● If you can't find a poem on a specific theme, then why not try writing one yourself?
● Read poems regularly to the children. Start with light, humorous poetry and then occasionally slip in more thoughtful pieces.
● If you are very keen, start a poetry club at your school.
● Invite an experienced teacher or visiting poet into your classroom.
● If you have a bookshop in your school, try to persuade the organiser to include specific poetry titles in the stock.
● Praise the children's efforts at writing poetry. We all enjoy success and are keen to work with and return to subjects that offer it.
● Above all, be enthusiastic about poetry! The teacher is an important role model for the children. If you are enthusiastic, the children will be keen as well.

The classroom

● Have you got a good selection of modern and traditional books in your classroom? Your local library service may be of help here.
● Set up a display of poetry books. This can be varied from a general collection to specific authors and themes.
● Make sure that there is a selection of dictionaries available which the children know how to use.
● Thesauruses are vital — try and obtain a set for the classroom or at least a set that can be shared with other classes.
● Put up wall displays of the children's poetic efforts regularly.
● Start a class poetry book which the children can organise and look through whenever they like.
● Put up a 'word of the day' and ask the children to bring in interesting words of their own. Encourage the children to look for words within words, for example, the word 'interest' also includes the words 'in' and 'rest'.
● Read jokes to the children and get them to retaliate! Encourage word play.
● Choose a 'poem of the week' and display it in the classroom.
● Start a top ten of favourite poetry books or poems. This can be changed every half-term or so.
● Have poetry tapes available. You can make your own or persuade a helpful parent to record some.
● Include poetry in the children's handwriting exercises.

The child

● Show and discuss with the children the various forms of poetry.
● Allow the children time to select and read poetry for themselves.

funny stupendous beautiful gigantic
wicked silly enormous tiny amazing

• Set a time aside for children to read poems aloud to the rest of the class. Can any of the children learn the poems off by heart? Keep a register of who has read – you can always allow the child who is a little shy to perform with a friend.
• Encourage the children to record their poems on tape. If they are very good the recordings can be added to your tape collections for everyone to hear.
• Encourage the children to keep a small book in which they can record ideas for poems.
• Use poems in assemblies and encourage choral reading
• Enter the children's poems in competitions.

WRITING POETRY

Before they start writing poetry, children should be given ample opportunity to read and listen to poetry. Let them listen to the rhythms and rhymes of poetry. Let them observe the patterns and shapes of poetry. Let them consider and discuss why a poet has written the poem in a particular way or has used the words and sounds in such a fashion. Where possible, make copies of the poems so that the children can see them, or if the children are near enough, let them read the poem with you. Through their close involvement of reading and listening to poetry, the children will become aware of, and in tune with, the variety of styles and options that are open to them when they come to write poems of their own.

The next stage is to encourage children to collect words.

Words!

I collect words
for there's a special net
inside my head
into which I pop:

interesting words,
silly words,
funny words,
nonsense words,
clever words,
difficult words,
creative words,
beautiful words,
and impressive words.

To me they are coins
saved for a special day,
occasionally to be taken out
and spent in a careful way!

Play word games with the children, have a word of the day, read jokes and puns, use thesauruses and dictionaries. Enthuse about words! Turn children into 'word watchers'!

A clear and keen awareness of the role children's senses can play in helping them to write is also paramount. Their senses need to be heightened to a level where they will intuitively use these perceptions and sensations as a creative working tool. Whether writing from first-hand or relying on notes or their imagination, children should be 'sensory aware'. They can be asked to exaggerate the image and then to look at it, touch it, smell it, listen to it and where appropriate, taste it. They can even give it human characteristics and become that object themselves.

As the children progress, introduce work on similes, metaphors and personification, stressing their importance and significance in descriptive work not only in poetry but also in prose. If these figures of speech are pointed out on a regular basis then, when the opportunity presents itself, they will become a natural part of the classroom vocabulary and writing, adding another dimension to the children's work as well as its subsequent quality.

The lesson

Every teacher has their own ideas on how the school day should be organised, but when writing (with children from around top infants upwards) it is important that all the children work together. This makes achieving the silence which is vital for the children when trying to create, so much easier. It also builds a sense of teamwork and 'writing togetherness' which in turn allows a certain quality to be achieved which is otherwise difficult to accomplish when various other activities are going on at the same time. However, if the whole class is to be involved in writing at the same time then you must usually allow two sessions if the work is to be completed satisfactorily. Also, if possible, try and train a parent to help.

The following is a checklist of ideas which may be of assistance when organising a poetry writing lesson.

First session

- Has the idea for the lesson been thought through properly? Is it suitable for the age group of the class? Could *you* write about it?
- Introduce and discuss the idea or topic with the children. Have you given the children prior notice so that they could consider the subject? For example, if writing a poem about 'night', the children could have taken helpful notes the previous evening or at least considered the topic.
- Read and share suitable poems and material. Where possible, children should have copies of the poems. (Remember they can be used time and time again!)
- Write plenty of vocabulary and ideas on the board.
- Explain that it is best to start a new line when there is a clear pause in the poem or the rhythm dictates it. Therefore, the children *must* read their poems over and over again to be aware of how their poem is developing in sound and shape. They should also be told that not every line need start with a capital letter or end with a comma — the choice usually lies with the poet!
- Initially, allow the children to write for five to twenty minutes in *silence*. (This will obviously depend on their age.)
- The children should have rough books, sharp pencils and access to an eraser. (If you wish they can also have word books to help them with spelling.)
- As the children write, circulate around the classroom passing helpful comments, but trying not to be too intrusive. Talk quietly to individuals, pointing out where new lines could begin or if capital letters are needed. The more you talk to the class the longer it will take to settle them down and concentrate on their writing.
- Children who have difficulty writing will obviously need a great deal of attention. You may have to be a scribe for them or let them record their words and ideas on tape. A helpful parent can be of great assistance in this situation.
- Try and play down the importance of spelling when drafting a poem, but if a child persists then you should insist that they try the word first in their word book. (About 50 per cent of the time junior-aged children will get the word correct!)
- Encourage the children to revise and proof-read their poems.
- When satisfied, the children should exchange their rough books with a critical friend (see Crafting and drafting).
- The critical friend should sign the book and return for amending.
- The work, still in rough but legible, can then be handed in for marking.

Second session

- The work is handed back to the children to be reread and your comments noted. At this stage time is always the thief! If a child wishes to develop or dramatically change a poem then he can take it home or spend lunch-times working on it. However, this is never easy as the timetable moves on.
- The children should write out their poems in final draft and decorate them if required. Word processing is always an option here, making use of various borders that a particular programme might offer.

• The children can present and read out their work to the rest of the class.

As soon as possible, some or all of the poems, should either be displayed or entered into a class poetry book.

CRAFTING AND DRAFTING

Crafting and drafting is a vital part of the poetry writing process. Even young children can do this by working with you via the board or a large sheet of paper. You can even make them aware of a rough first effort and its corrections. A poem by nature of its brevity can often be a help in this situation as there are fewer words to work with and therefore the whole process becomes simpler to manage and explain.

If the children in your class are new to drafting on their own, then show and explain to them that before we write we need to collect words and ideas. There are two ways of doing this: brainstorming (where you simply write down as many words or ideas as you can on a subject) and mind mapping (where you write the subject in the centre and flow out from it into smaller relating topics).

Brainstorming

storm
violent
loud
angry
booming
thunder
lightning
destruction
wind
rattling
rain
flooding
noisy . . .

Mind mapping

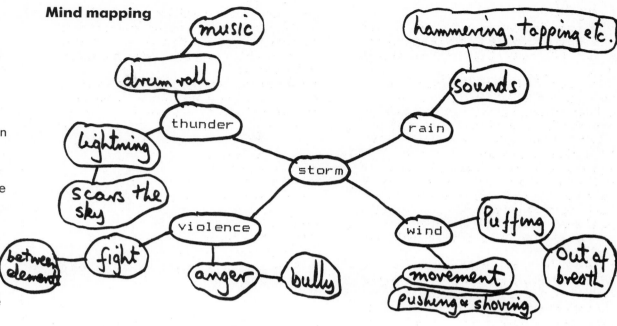

Once the children have written their poems in draft form they need to find a 'voice' to help them consider their work. As the teacher is not always available and to promote their own revising skills, it is helpful to provide a list of questions for them to ask themselves as a guide-line. The questions will obviously vary with the age of the children. However, do not expect too much – revising is a difficult skill that will take some time to develop.
• Have you said everything you wanted to say?
• How does your poem read and sound?
• Have you included new vocabulary or any comparisons?
• Underline any words you feel could be more interesting and by using your thesaurus see if you can change them.

• If you have written in rhyme or used a pattern have you kept this going all the way through the poem?
• Have you used a new line when you want a pause in the poem?
• Is your ending good enough?
• Will the poem interest the reader?
• Have you proof-read the poem checking for meaning, spelling and punctuation?

Once the children are satisfied with their efforts they need to exchange their poems with a critical partner – a friend who is willing to share and offer *positive* praise and criticism, writing a comment of reasonable length about the poem. Again, this is a skill that takes time to nurture but the following questions may help.
• Do you understand the poem?
• Which part did you enjoy the most?

- Are there any parts that could be improved?
- Are there any parts that could be shortened, left out or set out in a different way?
- Are there any mistakes with spelling, grammar or punctuation?

The last question is always a difficult one, for while chidlren will happily help each other with spelling, the grammatical and punctuation side is formidable. The starting of a line with a capital letter or the placing of commas and full stops is very much up to the individual poet. However, it is beneficial to make the children look out for problems of grammar – there just might be the odd glaring error or two that they can assist each other with!

Before the children appraise each other's poems it is a good idea first to do several critical appraisals on the board with the whole class – perhaps using your own work. For those teachers who feel a little daunted at this prospect it is not as difficult as it may sound. Go with what feels natural and you will all learn together.

The teacher's role in responding to the children's work will reflect much of what has been outlined. She will be involved in setting up 'writing interviews' where she should look for the positive and then guide with subtle hints and pointers. (The following example may be of some enlightenment in what can be achieved with crafting and drafting.)

The first stage with Jamie's poem has been his mind map which is wonderfully detailed. Obviously this form of collecting information suited him very well and he also enjoyed the process. Other children may prefer to make a list of ideas and occasionally some children prefer to start writing their poem straight out and then brainstorm or mind map for further information.

Jamie's Draft Poem

MY ROOM!

My ROOM is yellow
Stacked high with books,
toys, teddys, posters and ~~dores~~ RUBBISH.
I have a desk full of RUBBISH.
Bins full to the brim
Photos on the wall
I also have a dark cupboard
I am scared of it.
A pin-board is full of cadges
By my bed.

Your choice as regards capitals →

My ROOM.

(Jamie – Can you try and put in a comparison?)

? bedroom ?

My room (lemon) ↑walls.
Has yellow
A (better word?) big door.
And (old) ⊙ boxes piled high.
Curtains shaded (brilliant) green,
Board games all over the floor.
Bins full of rubbish (?) to the brim,
Annuals and comics put neatly on my shelf.

And also a (glowing) spinning chair.
Books and a (adj) lamp on my chest of drawers
Teddy tucked (adj) up in my bed nice and warm,
And I alsohave a creepy cupboard.
⊳ I like my room ~~that~~
⊳ I think – – – – –   :-)
(Can you think of a more satisfactory ending) By: Jamie Thomson
I like the poem because it tell you about
it and the poem makes me feel I am
in it. The best bit about poem that I like is
The books and the glowing lamp. George White

Jamie's next stage has been his draft poem which was appraised by his critical partner George. The positive remark of 'the poem makes me feel I am in it', was an excellent observation and what better compliment could Jamie have asked for? The work was then handed to the teacher and discussed with both oral and written comments provided. This is not always possible and sometimes the comments are all written. (The oral comments on the poem are shown in brackets and these were mutually agreed.)

The final version of 'My bedroom' was written out in Jamie's English book where it was marked. It was praised and he was keen to read it to the rest of the class.

My Bedroom

My bedroom
Has lemon yellow walls,
A massive white shining door,
And old boxes piled high.
Curtains shaded brilliant green,
Board games scattered all over the floor
Bins full of rubbish topped to the brim.
Annuals and comics put neatly on my shelf,
And also a spinning chair.
Books and a glowing lamp on my chest of drawers.
Teddy tucked up in my bed nice and warm.
I also have a creepy cupboard,
Like a dark, secret cave.
I like my room,
I think it was made just for me!

By: Jamie Thomson

PRESENTATION AND DISPLAY

Drama and music can obviously be incorporated in some of the poetry ideas listed in this book. Drama can be especially useful when introducing topics where emotions are being considered. If children act out the chosen subject, in groups or in pairs, they can go some way to experiencing the emotion for themselves. Music can assist with emphasising rhythms and helping to add an extra, stimulating dimension to the poetry lesson.

We should be aiming to make poetry a listening and speaking experience as well as a writing and reading one. When presenting poetry to an audience there are a few golden rules for the speaker whether child or adult.

- Never start until everybody is listening.
- Make sure you have prepared everything you are to read. The poems will flow much more easily.
- You can involve the audience by allowing them to guess certain rhymes in a poem or join in with a repeated chorus.
- Speak clearly and where necessary vary your voice and pace. Remember the audience does not generally have the advantage of seeing the words and will need time to digest what you are saying!
- Do not be frightened of reading a poem several times or going back to one a week later. Your audience will often notice and appreciate different points.
- If you are reading a lot of poetry, try to vary the choice of your material.

Display can also play an important part in creating a positive attitude towards poetry in the classroom. The following are just a few ideas that might be of help.

- The children can make a poster advertising their favourite poem or poetry book.
- Let the children write out a favourite

poem for a handwriting exercise. These poems can then be decorated and displayed in the classroom.
- Make a class poetry book where the poems from displays are put — when they are taken down — together with any other work the class would wish to include.
- Devise a class poetry board for all sorts of poems, jokes and word play.
- Make a poet-tree. The children can write their poems on leaves to be placed on the tree. The tree can also be decorated with flowers, insects and birds.
- Let the children choose a favourite poem and write it inside the decorated shape of a kite. They can attach the titles of other favourite poems or poets to the tail.

POETS IN SCHOOL

No matter how well you read poetry, how well you enthuse and teach the subject, there is always something extra special when an experienced and enthusiastic poet visits your school.

If you are wondering how to organise such an event, then your local Regional Arts Board (see the Resources section) will recommend poets in your area and may well subsidise part of the costs, but apply early as funds are limited. The Poetry Society (see the Resources section) organise a Poets in School Scheme which is funded by W. H. Smith. This scheme organises a poet to make three visits to your school and to work with groups of children. The final visit usually culminates in an evening performance of the children's work. It is also possible to try and approach individual poets themselves and addresses can usually be obtained via the poet's publisher.

A poet might be invited into your school for a variety of reasons. It may be to stimulate poetry in the school, to work with a particular age group, to talk about being a poet and a writer or to join in a poetry/book week. For whatever reason you invite a poet to visit your school, remember to consider the following.

- Is the poet's work and approach conducive to your needs?
- If required, can the poet cope with an infant age group? (Ring your Arts Board or The Poetry Society to discuss.)
- Discuss what the poet is prepared to do, for example, readings and workshops, and how he/she will organise the session.
- What resources and space will the poet require?
- Do all the staff know of the visit and the day's timetable? Is it going to be quiet in the right place at the right time?
- Do the children and the rest of the staff know of the poet's work? The children may also like to consider questions to ask.
- Discuss costs with the poet, for example travelling expenses and whether a school meal is required.

- Well in advance of the visit, send the poet a map of how to get to the school and a detailed timetable for the day.
- Will the poet bring any of his books to sell? If so, how much will the books cost?

USING THIS BOOK

There are three main sections in this book which deal with teaching ideas and activities. The first – 'Warming up' – is intended to provide an introduction to poetry. The activities are geared towards catching the children's attention and stimulating their involvement by using enjoyable word fun and rhyming activities.

The activities in 'Poetry in motion' are concerned with writing poems of greater length and substance. They also introduce the concepts of more formal poetry.

'Topical poetry' contains a selection of poetry ideas that relate to specific teaching topics. However, these ideas can also be used independently.

In all three sections an age range guide is offered for each activity, but obviously this is merely a guide and activities can easily be adapted to suit the requirements of all children. The teaching style advocated in this book is a whole class approach. This means that unless otherwise stated children will be working as a whole class. Where this is not applicable the appropriate group size has been indicated. This also applies to materials needed to complete activities. For most activities all that is required is a pencil, paper and eraser and possibly a good thesaurus – where other materials are required this is mentioned in the text under the heading 'What you need'.

This book also provides a variety of structures and frameworks as an aid to encouraging children to write poetry. These ideas are not mandatory. They are there to be used, adapted or ignored to fit the children's and teachers' needs. However, never lose sight of the fact that writing, although rewarding, is hard work! There can be immense satisfaction gained by completing that poem, but this satisfaction has to be earned. For children taking their first steps into poetry the whole process can be rather daunting and the help these activities offer is somewhat of a handrail that will hopefully lead up the poetic staircase. At some stage on their journey it is hoped that the children will learn to manage without the rail and eventually reach the door of poetry. The door, no matter how big or small, once reached and entered will remain firmly open in their minds for the rest of their lives.

Inside a poem

It doesn't always have to rhyme,
but there's the repeat of a beat,
somewhere
an inner chime that makes you want to
tap your feet or swerve in a curve;
a lilt, a leap, a lightning-split:
thunderstruck the consonants jut,
while the vowels open wide as waves in
    the noon-blue sea.
You hear with your heels, your eyes feel
what they never touched before:
fins on a bird, feathers on a deer;
taste all colours, inhale
memory and tomorrow and always the
    tang is today.

Eve Merriam

Warming up

Nursery rhymes

Age range
Four to five.

What you need
Large sheet of paper or flip chart.

What to do
Sit down with the children round you and start reading out traditional nursery rhymes. As you read each rhyme, write down the title on a large piece of paper. This sheet should be retained in the classroom and the children encouraged to bring in their favourite rhymes to add to the classroom list. Once this list of nursery rhymes has grown a little, the children can be challenged to try and recite some of the nursery rhymes on the list either with a friend on their own.

This activity makes sure that all the children have an awareness and a reasonable understanding of what a nursery rhyme is, as well as introducing them to the written language of the titles.

Finally, the children could vote on a top ten of favourite nursery rhymes.

Have you ever seen?

Age range
Four to five.

What to do
This is a simple nonsense game involving rhyme. Ask the children to think of an object or item and then find a rhyming doing word for the item, for example:
- Have you ever seen butter mutter?
- Have you ever seen a fly cry?
- Have you ever seen a chip flip?
- Have you ever seen a drink wink?
The sillier the better!

Nursery rhyme fun

Age range
Four to seven.

What to do
Encourage the children to recite, enjoy and familiarise themselves with the following nursery rhymes:
- 'Baa, baa black sheep';
- 'Hickory, dickory, dock';
- 'Polly put the kettle on'.
  Now ask the children to try changing some of the lyrics in these rhymes, for example:
- Baa, baa red sheep (green, white, yellow and so on),
  Have you any jelly (grass, snow, bananas and so on)?
  Yes, sir, yes, sir,
  Three plates (sacks, dishes, bowls and so on) full.
- Hickory, dickory, dock,
  The mouse ran up the clock.
  The clock struck two (three, four and so on),
  The mouse shouted, 'Boo!'
  (WHEEEE!, fell to the floor and so on).
  Hickory, dickory, dock.

- Susan put the kettle on (use class names),
  Susan put the kettle on,
  Susan put the kettle on,
  And we all have strawberry milkshakes (fizzy lemonade and so on)!
  David take it off again,
  David take it off again,
  David take it off again,
  They've tumbled down the stairs (fallen off to sleep and so on)!

Follow-up
With older children you can ask them to write out their new versions of the rhymes and any of their own ideas. After further discussion let them word-play with their own choice of nursery rhymes.

I spy a rhyme

Age range
Five to seven.

Group size
The whole class, small groups or pairs.

What to do
This is a quick five minute idea that can be used to sharpen the children's rhyming skills. It is based on the traditional 'I Spy' game. The wording is simply altered to 'I spy with my little eye a word that rhymes with . . .' and the children hopefully reply with their own rhyming responses. For example, if the word is 'black' the children may respond with 'sack'.

This game can be organised as a competition working with the whole class, working in teams or, if you prefer it a little more subdued, then let the children work in pairs where they ask each other.

Old MacDonald had a school

Age range
Five to seven.

What to do
Use the lyrics and tune from Old MacDonald but alter the lyrics to suit your school or class. A typical rendition might go something as follows:

Mr Souter had a class,
E...I...E...I...O
And in his class,
He had Jamie Adams,
E...I...E...I...O
With a laugh, laugh here,
And a laugh, laugh there,
Here a laugh,
There a laugh,
Everywhere a laugh, laugh.
Mr Souter had a class,
E...I...E...I...O

The children hugely enjoy singing about various members of the class and providing it is done in a positive way it generally works very well.

Rhyme clap

Age range
Five to eight.

What you need
Photocopiable pages 113 and 114.

What to do
Rhyme clapping will help the children to familiarise themselves with rhyming words. Use the rhyming word sheets to select key words and then call out rhyming and non-rhyming words. Tell the children to clap when they hear a word that rhymes with the key word, but not to clap when it does not rhyme.

When the children are confident with the idea and the sheet they could take turns to lead the game.

Rhyme slime!

Age range
Five to eight.

What to do
Mention mud to children and you get various reactions — the occasional groan but mostly shouts of enjoyment. Sometimes you'll notice a child lost inside her imagination as she mimes squelching and wallowing in the stuff. Children certainly enjoy hearing about mud as should be evident on reading 'The mud-pie makers rhyme' below. This poem is excellent for discussing rhyme and onomatopoeia — 'oozey-woozey' and so on.

The mud-pie makers rhyme

Mud is squidgy,
slippery, sludgey.
Mud is irmy-squirmy goo.
Mud is runny,
squeezy, funny.
Mud is oozey-woozey too.

Mud you can roll flat,
mud you can press.
Mud is the nicest, muddiest mess.
Mud you can make with,
mud you can share.
Our mud-pies are the best anywhere.

Mud is squidgy,
slippery, sludgey.
Mud is irmy-squirmy goo.
Mud is runny,
squeezy, funny.
Mud is oozey-woozey too.

Janet Paisley

Finally, ask the children to make up their own words to describe mud, for example, dunky, squoochy, swiggly, wumpy. Hopefully everyone will have almost as much fun inventing new squelching words as they have playing with the mud itself. Eventually, the children should have an attempt at writing their own mud poem or with very young children you could be the scribe for a 'muddy' class poem.

Try and arrange to have some mud laid out in a suitable area for the children to 'thud mud'! (Make sure the children wear disposable gloves when handling mud.) After reading the poem discuss what other words the children could use in describing mud and playing with it, for example, sloppy, squelchy, soggy, squirty and so on. Then see if they can imitate the double rhymes in the poem with descriptions of their own — squelchy-welchy, slippy-sloppy, boggy-soggy.

Body rhymes

Age range
Five to nine.

What you need
Photocopiable page 116.

What to do
First the children need to discuss names for various body parts. write these names out on the board. Younger children can have fun just discussing their ideas. Older children can use the words in their own body poems, for example:

On my chest,
There is a bird's nest.
On my toe,
there is a sign saying 'NO!'.
On my bones,
There are telephones . . .

The rhyme wheel on photocopiable page 116 can be fun to use with this activity, providing the children are of sufficient ability.

Imagine

Age range
Five to nine.

What you need
Photocopiable page 116.

What to do
This activity is an excellent way of allowing children to develop the use of the simile while at the same time having a lot of fun with rhyme. The children have simply to use their imaginations and come up with as unusual and as amusing a comparison as they can possibly imagine. As in the example shown it should of course be written in rhyme and the children should find the rhyme wheel on photocopiable page 116 helpful. With the younger children this can be carried out as an enjoyable oral activity.

Imagine a horse
as big as a golf course.

Imagine a hen
as thin as a pen.

Imagine a cow
taking a bow.

Imagine a fly
dressed as a spy.

Imagine a house
shaped like a mouse.

Imagine the sky
covered in apple pie.

Just imagine!

I wish

Age range
Six to eight.

Group size
Whole class and pairs.

What to do
Children love the poem 'I wish'. They enjoy the rhyme,
the silliness and the word play of it. They love to join in
and recite it with you.

I wish

Oh I wish I was a little drop of mud,
Oh I wish I was a little drop of mud,
I'd oozy and I'd squoozy
under everybody's shoesy,
Oh I wish I was a little drop of mud.

Oh I wish I was a little cake of soap,
Oh I wish I was a little cake of soap,
I's slippy and I'd slidey
under everybody's hidey,
Oh I wish I was a little cake of soap.

Oh I wish I was a little drop of water,
Oh I wish I was a little drop of water,
I'd squirty all the dirty
under everybody's shirty,
Oh I wish I was a little drop of water.

Oh I wish I was a little mosquito,
Oh I wish I was a little mosquito,
I'd hidey and I'd bitey
under everybody's nightie,
Oh I wish I was a little mosquito.

Oh I wish I was a little tickly sneeze,
Oh I wish I was a little tickly sneeze,
I'd itchy and I'd twitchy
under everybody's snitchy,
Oh I wish I was a tickly sneeze.

Oh I wish I was a fishy in the sea,
Oh I wish I was a fishy in the sea,
I'd swim around so cute
without a bathing suit,
Oh I wish I was a fishy in the sea.

(Adapted by Ian Souter)

Once you have gone through the poem enough times for the children to know it, you can throw the session open for a few minutes and allow them to try and make up their own verses. This can be a little chaotic but fun. Older children could then try and write a verse or two of their own. Initially, it is best if you do one verse with the whole class. It can be done on the board as a cloze procedure exercise with the children filling in the missing words.

Oh I wish I was a little feather,
Oh I wish I was a little feather,
I'd _____ and I'd _____, (trickly, stickly)
under everybody's _____. (tickly)

Other possible subjects to suggest to the children are: bird, bee, ant, sweet, machine, teddy.

Ready steady rhyme!

Age range
Six to nine.

Group size
Pairs.

What you need
Photocopiable pages 113 and 114.

What to do
For this activity the children need to use the rhyme sheet on photocopiable pages 113 and 114. Let the children work in pairs. Tell them to pick out and agree a key word from the rhyming sheet or you may give them a suitable word. They should then turn the sheet over and as fast as they can, write down as many words that rhyme with the key word as possible. Once they have finished they can check each other's lists to see who has thought of the most rhyming words.

Finally, ask the children to make up sentences using as many of their words as they can. The sentences can be as silly as they want, but they must make reasonable sense, for example, 'There was a shock for a sock when it was knocked and locked in a clock'.

Ten huge hippos
Swinging on the line.
Ten huge hippos
Swinging on the line.
And if one huge hippo
Should swing out just too far, there'd be
Nine huge hippos,
Jumping on the line,
Nine huge hippos,
Jumping on the line
And if one huge hippo
Should . . .

Ten

Age range
Six to nine.

What to do
We all know the nursery rhyme 'Ten green bottles'. Why not have a spot of fun and instead of singing about bottles use various creatures? The children can either finish the rhyme below or write out their own. Remember to point out the rhyming pattern.

Encourage the children to describe their creatures with adjectives that are alliterative, for example, wobbling wasps, dangerous dragons and so on. If ten is too many you could obviously start with the number of your choice.

Once the children have written their poems they can read or sing them.

Expanding sentences

Age range
Six to nine.

Group size
Pairs.

What to do
Ask the children to make up a simple sentence. They should then work with a partner and take turns to expand the sentence until they can go no further. The last person to write a sentence is the winner; for example:
- Sally sat on the chair.
- Sad Sally sat on the chair.
- Sad Sally sat on the black chair.
- Sad Sally who was upset sat on the black chair.
- Sad Sally who was upset sat on the black chair and cried.

Stepping up

Age range
Six to nine.

What to do
The aim of this activity is to develop the children's concentration and descriptive powers with relation to a single topic. Ask the children to choose a noun and then see how tall they can make their poem by stepping up the page using single words that in some way relate to the topic; for example:

                              burst!
                        throw,
                    catch,
                plastic,
            red,
        round,
    bounce,
Ball,

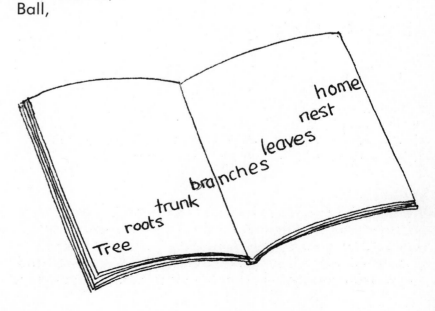

Word mixing

Age range
Six to nine.

What you need
Dictionaries, thesauruses, 12cm × 10cm pieces of card, thick felt-tipped pens, string, hole punch.

What to do
Ask the children to find interesting words from their dictionaries, thesauruses or, if you prefer, topic words. Encourage the children to choose words that have other words within them such as 'foresight' — for, fore, or and sight. With younger children you may need to restrict the number of letters they use and the children could work in pairs.

Give the children rectangular pieces of card — one card for each letter in their word. Ask them to print out clearly each letter of the word on both sides of the card — one letter for each card. The children will have to write the word in reverse order when doing the backs of the cards. It is best to ask the children to do it in pencil first and then have it checked. They can decorate the letters with a border, but stress that the letters should stand out clearly.

Finally, the words can be strung across the classroom. Punch one hole at the top of each card so that the cards will turn freely. Now stand back and watch as an amazing array of words spin in and out of sequence.

Back to front

Age range
Seven to eleven.

Group size
Pairs.

What to do
Ask the children to write down words but to write the letters in reverse order so that the words read 'back to front'. The children should try to write whole sentences in this way but they should not reverse the word order — that can come at a later stage for those who wish to try. When the sentences are written the children can exchange them with a partner and the first to unravel the meaning is the winner. Encourage the children to 'taeb rieht rentrap'!

THE CRYING TELEPHONE SKIED DOWN THE ESCALATOR..

What a load of nonsense!

Age range
Seven to nine.

What you need
Photocopiable page 115.

What to do
Make sure that each child has a copy of photocopiable page 115. They should use the sheet to write five silly and nonsensical sentences. All they have to do is choose a word from each column in order, but from any row; for example, 'The orange baby climbed a banana'.

Once the children have written five nonsense sentences they could use the blank table to make up their own. They will need help with the order of nouns, verbs and adjectives.

Fuddle and muddle

Age range
Seven to eleven.

Group size
Pairs.

What you need
Strips of paper, scissors.

What to do
Ask the children to write out a sentence on a strip of paper, using the appropriate punctuation – capital letters, full stops, question marks and so on. They should then cut their sentences up into individual words and swap their words with a friend. The children should now try to put the sentences back together again.

Flick and pick

Age range
Seven to eleven.

Group size
Pairs.

What you need
Dictionaries.

What to do
Ask the children to flick through their dictionaries and choose three or four words that interest them. The words chosen must include a noun and a verb. They should then work with a partner to make up sentences using their words. For example, if they choose the words hen, lemonade, diamonds, squashing, they might make up a sentence like 'The lemonade hen was squashing diamonds'.

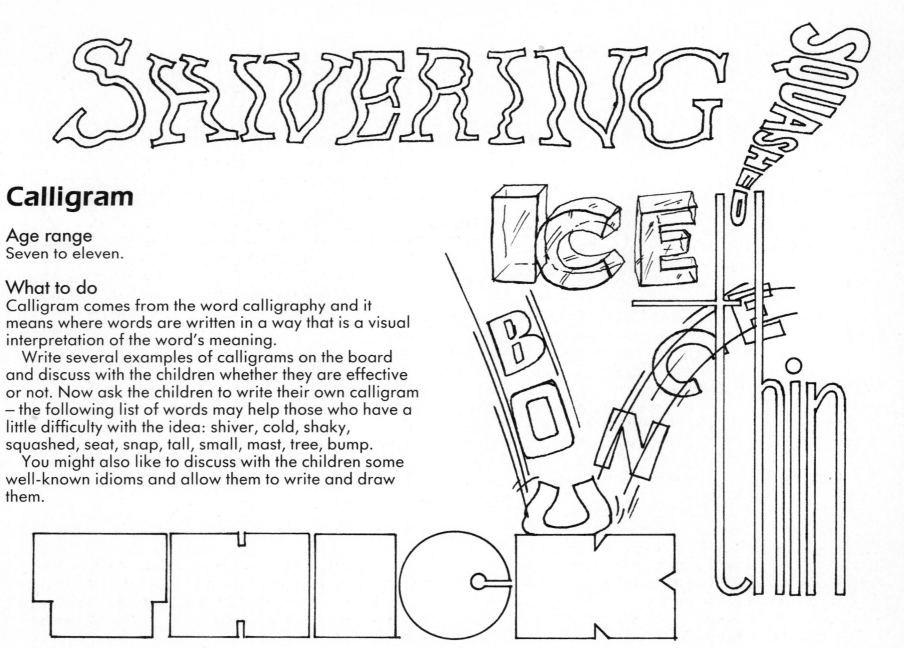

Calligram

Age range
Seven to eleven.

What to do
Calligram comes from the word calligraphy and it means where words are written in a way that is a visual interpretation of the word's meaning.

Write several examples of calligrams on the board and discuss with the children whether they are effective or not. Now ask the children to write their own calligram – the following list of words may help those who have a little difficulty with the idea: shiver, cold, shaky, squashed, seat, snap, tall, small, mast, tree, bump.

You might also like to discuss with the children some well-known idioms and allow them to write and draw them.

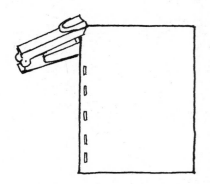

1. Staple sheets of paper together.

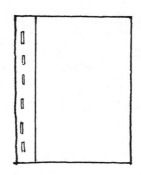

2. Draw a margin parallel to staples.

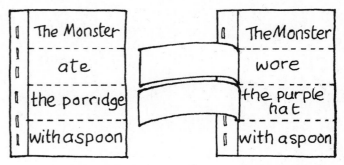

3. Divide each page horizontally into four by drawing dotted lines for each part of the sentence.

4. Cut along each dotted line so that the sections can be flipped back in different combinations.

Mixed up fun

Age range
Eight to eleven.

What you need
Scrap paper, stapler, scissors.

What to do
Children enjoy changing the order of phrases or words in a sentence. Ask the children to invent an interesting first line and then just mix up the words:
- The men trained the parrot to talk.
- The parrot trained the men to talk.
- The trained men talk to the parrot.

The children can make up their own word-mixing books. First staple four A4 or A5 size sheets of scrap paper together. Now ask the children to draw a margin down the side of their books parallel to the staples and then horizontally divide each page into quarters, drawing dotted lines on each page. Next ask the children to make up four sentences in the following format:

The monster	ate	the porridge	with a spoon.
(noun)	(verb)	(noun)	(object/instrument)

The children should write one sentence on each page so that each part is written in each of the four sections. The children should then cut along each line on all the pages and then they can flip the sections to make up lots of hilarious sentences.

Poetry in motion

The comparison game

Age range
Five to eleven.

What to do
The usage of the simile and metaphor in developing the quality of children's writing is vital. This activity is intended to help children develop this usage.

Choose a subject with which all the children have had some first-hand experience; 'weather' is an ideal topic. Write a few lines of a descriptive poem on the topic making sure you use lots of similes and metaphors, for example:

> The fog is like a magician's cape
> making objects disappear.
> It is like a cold, grey monster
> swallowing whole houses as it goes.

Ask the children to use this poem's structure and attempt to write their own poems or you could act as scribe on a whole class effort.

When they have written their poems let the children read them out. Ask them to try taking away the word 'like' and discuss with the children whether it makes any difference to their poems. Do they prefer it? Does it paint a clearer picture in the reader/listener's mind?

Ask the children to try writing on another topic but this time without using the word 'like'.

Love my pet

Age range
Six to eight.

What to do

Love my dog!

Love me, love my dog
I always say,
for unfortunately he:

wacks people with his tail
when he is pleased to see them,

pushes those who get too close
into the park boating lake,

chases the garden frogs
out of their watery home in the pond,

races our poor rabbit
around the garden until she's exhausted,

bites everything in sight
including the cat's tail,

eats the morning newspaper
until it lies in tattered shreds,

sniffs anything and everything that moves
as if he's a vacuum cleaner on legs,

pounds all over my bed
ESPECIALLY when I'm in it and peacefully asleep,

kisses everyone with his tongue
as though he's wiping them with a wet sponge.

But best of all
when Dad plays his 'boogie-woogie' music,
he rears up, presents his paws
and off we go dancing across the floor!

Love me, love my dog
I always say
because I certainly do!

For very young children you could write down their ideas and then work together to make a whole class poem. This poem could then be typed out and displayed in the classroom.

The children could also be encouraged to bring in photographs of their pets. Not only would this stimulate discussion, but some photographs could be placed next to the final poems allowing the children to consider whether their poems actually reflect the true appearance of their pets.

Read the above poem to the children. They will probably be keen to share with the class their own pets' peculiarities. Now all you need to do is channel this enthusiasm into a list poem. A good idea is to start the poem with 'my cat', or whatever the pet is, and then ask the children to write their thoughts, beginning each idea with an action (verb). They can finish their poems by saying what they feel about their pet, for example:

My cat,
jumps on . . .,
trips up . . .,
meows at . . .
My cat makes me laugh!

Daddy in bed

Age range
Six to eight.

What to do

Daddy in bed

When Daddy was in bed
It was very early.
He didn't wake up
So I shouted at him,
He still didn't wake up
So I jumped on him,
He still didn't wake up
So I pulled the quilt off him,
He still didn't wake up
So I tickled his feet,
He still didn't wake up
So I wiped him with a wet sponge,
He still didn't wake up
So I sprayed him with perfume,
He still didn't wake up
But he smelled nice.

Natasha Gammon (Age 6)

This poem, when well read, usually has the class in fits of giggles — so why not use the poem's structure and the children's attraction to it to get them writing? This can stretch their imagination by substituting anyone or a creature in the place of Daddy, for example:

When the cat was asleep (or the dog, my sister and so on)
I . . .
She didn't wake up
So I . . .
She still didn't wake up
So I . . .

Encourage the children to make up their own endings.

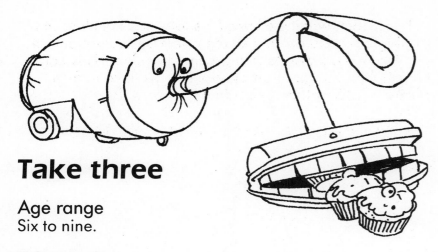

Take three

Age range
Six to nine.

What to do
Choose a general topic such as animals, weather, transport, machines and so on. The children now need to draw three columns. Tell them that they must write suitable objects from the topic in the middle column, words that describe the object in the first column, and a word to describe what the objects is doing in the third column; for example:

In my house

noisy	washing machines	spinning
angry	kettles	steaming
white	fridges	humming
hungry	hoovers	sucking

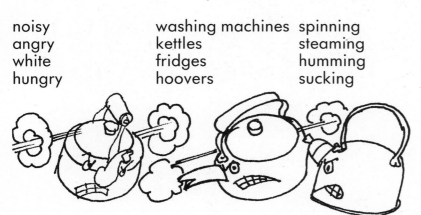

Now magically the children will have the ingredients for a poem.

In my house

There are,
noisy washing machines spinning,
angry kettles steaming,
white fridges humming,
hungry hoovers sucking
and I can't sleep!

The last line is optional but it helps to round the poem off. Usually, the suggestions of 'and . . .' leads the children to think of their own acceptable last line.

Watch out!

Age range
Six to nine.

What to do
This activity is intended to help improve awareness and encourage children's powers of observation. After playtime secretly ask two children to stay outside the classroom when the rest of the class return. Tell the class that they must think hard and try to describe the appearance of the two missing children. Can they remember what the two children are wearing? This can produce peals of laughter especially when the children return to the room and the class realise how wrong they have been. However, it is important that descriptions are positive and not too personal.

If you want the children to write, then the next stage is to ask them for a description of someone such as the headteacher or the teacher who has taken the assembly that morning. Make sure that the person being described is able and willing to come into the classroom at a specific time later that day so that the children can see how accurately they have been able to describe their appearance.

This activity can be used, with older children, as an interesting way in developing the children's awareness of the difference between prose and poetry. With older children it might be a good idea to let them write their initial description in prose and then write it again, at a later stage, as a descriptive poem. An easier option is for you to write a short description of a child in prose on the board and then, with the children's help, transpose it into a poem.

Alliteration by number

Age range
Six to nine.

What you need
Dictionaries.

What to do
Alliteration is where words of the same sound are grouped together. The effect is generally pleasing to the ear and fun.

Ask the children to write ten alliterative sentences using the numbers one to ten to begin each sentence. They should take the initial letter sound from each number and use their dictionaries to help them find other words, for example:

One wet, waterproofed, wasp wobbled and whistled.
Two troublesome taxi drivers tackled Tarzan.
Three . . .

Follow-up
The children can make an alliterative alphabet book. Give each child a letter and tell them to make up any alliterative sentence with this letter. They can decorate their sentences and place them in a class book for all to share and read. Depending on the numbers in the class, the letters may have to be shared between some children.

Three thin, thoughtful teachers.

Four fat, famous fighters.

Six slim, sassy singers.

One wet, waterproofed wasp.

I remember being really stupid when:

I was learning to ride a bike
and I rode over the cat's tail.
He turned into a rocket
and shot through the hedge.
Then I set off
to climb the garden tree
and half-way up —
I got stuck!

Memories

Age range
Six to eleven.

What to do
We all have memories and this activity provides an ideal
opportunity to first remember and then to write about
them. The poem 'I remember' serves as a starting point
which should stimulate the children to talk about their
clearest memories. The key here is to get the children to
describe the reason why the memory is so clear.

I remember being really fed up when:

We moved to a new house
and I lost my favourite, old teddy
then I found my music box had been broken.
The very next day,
I was playing hide and seek,
I hid behind the curtains
and somehow I managed —
to pull them all down!

I remember really having the giggles when:

My baby brother
got his head stuck in the cat flap.
We couldn't get him out
and had to call the fire brigade.
Then mum tried to put a shelf up
in my newly decorated bedroom
and when she wasn't looking —
it fell on her head!

Explain the structure of the poem to the children. The idea is that two memories are covered in each verse and reasons should be given. Ask the children to think of an emotion such as being angry, jealous, happy and so on. They must then think of a memory they have which is connected with that emotion. Why is the memory so clear to them? They should then use the structure of the poem to write their own efforts. You can write the first line on the board to help them if you like.

'I remember feeling really angry when:'

If working with younger children you may want to ask them to write any one idea per emotion while older children could attempt two.

I remember really feeling guilty when:

I was supposed to be watching my littler sister
and she shot over to our washing machine
opened the door and fell in!
Then I tried to help my brother
with his loose tooth.
But instead of pulling it out
I pushed it in and –
he swallowed it!

Yes I certainly do remember!

Tongue twisters

Age range
Six to eleven.

What to do
The day before you do this activity, ask the children to search for tongue twisters. They may often find one in a joke book or someone in the family may remember an old favourite.

Tongue twisters by the sheer weight of repetition of sounds are extremely difficult to read and you usually end up laughing. They need to be read fast and at least twice, to fully appreciate the 'tongue twisting'.

In starting the activity it is a good idea to have five or six tongue twisters already written out on the board. The children can then enjoy themselves reading them out aloud; for example:
- Red leather, yellow leather.
- Bad black bran bread.
- Does double bubble gum double bubble?
- Moses supposes his toeses are roses.
- How much caramel can a canny cannibal cram in a camel?
- Peter poked a poker at the piper, so the piper poked pepper at Peter.

Tommy tends to knot his tongue when tackling the toughest twisters.

The children can also tell each other the tongue twisters they found themselves. Discuss with them what they feel makes a good tongue twister and ask them to try and write their own. You can help the children to do this by supplying them with the following beginnings to get them started:
- Sunny sunshine . . .
- Crazy Masie . . .
- The ship slipped . . .
- Can Dan . . .
- Which wicked witch . . .

Follow-up

Hold a competition to find the best tongue twister. Older children can try reading the poem 'The wizard and the lizard'. At first they should read it slowly and then as quickly as their tongues will allow!

The wizard and the lizard

Once a wizard in a blizzard
caught a lizard down a well.
First he took it, then he shook it,
Did he cook it? Time will tell.

How he spluttered as he muttered,
till he spluttered out a spell.
Then, hey presto! Full of zest, O,
Have you guessed, O do not yell!

It was tragic that his magic
Word Kadagic wasn't right,
For the lizard in the blizzard
Gave the wizard quite a fright.

It grew larger than a Rajah,
With a barge, a butt, a bite,
First it fizzled, till it grizzled,
then it sizzled out of sight!

Colin West

The challenge is now on for the children to write their own tongue twister poem.

Sensible stuff

Age range
Seven to ten.

What to do
This is a simple idea which intermingles senses and emotions in a poetic form. It also offers, if you so wish, less able or less experienced children a structure to help guide them in their writing.

Initially, read the children a variety of poems which express a strong emotion and discuss these as a class. Emotions such as fear, happiness, jealousy, anger, love and sadness offer a rewarding springboard for classroom discussion. Anger is always a very productive area in which to work as all children have memories of someone being annoyed with them or vice versa. The children may also benefit from role-play work.

After the reading and discussion ask the children to write. Give them the following questions as guidelines:
- What colour is your emotion?
- What does it look, smell, sound, taste, feel like?
- How does it move?
- Does it remind you of the weather or an animal?
- How does your body change with this emotion?
- How do you feel when it has gone?

Bear in mind that this structure is meant to be flexible and that the children can use all, some or none of the questions to help with their poems and in any order they wish. For those children who are struggling, it offers a much needed help and for those who have a clear idea, then it may just help develop or stimulate an idea.

To avoid the children beginning each line with 'Anger is . . .' ask them to alternate between 'Anger is . . .' and the pronoun 'it' or encourage them to use the name of the emotion in the title and the first line only.

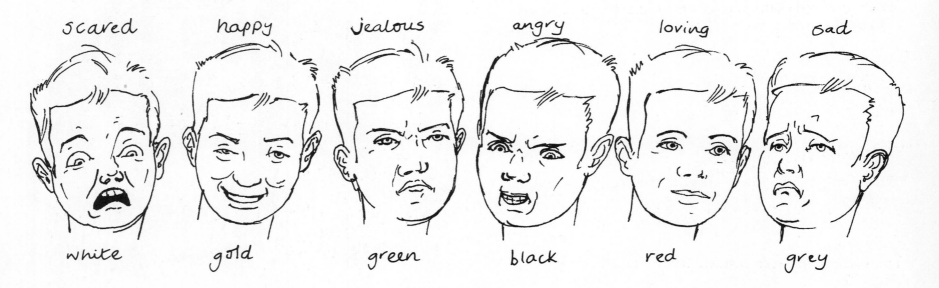

scared — white   happy — gold   jealous — green   angry — black   loving — red   sad — grey

The furniture game

Age range
Seven to eleven.

What to do
The furniture game is played by the children thinking of somebody – friend, brother, sister, parent, teacher or famous person – and describing them under the following headings:
- a colour;
- a pet;
- type of weather;
- article of clothing;
- piece of furniture;
- a television programme;
- a suitable meal.

   When writing the poem the children should choose a person they like and write in a pleasant, positive fashion, initially keeping to the structure shown in the example:

Gran

Gran is pink,
She is a labrador.
Gran is a sunny day,
She is an old sweater.
Gran is a rocking chair,
She is Coronation Street.
Gran is fish fingers and
chips with tomato sauce!

Follow-up
To develop this idea a stage further see 'Family' on page 92.

My Brother

My brother is
brown
He's a gerbil
He's a rainy day
An old shoe
A kitchen chair, solid and square
He's Tomorrow's World not Top
of the Pops
A full plate of cabbage that
nobody eats.

Louder than . . .

Age range
Seven to eleven.

What you need
The first verse of 'Louder than a clap of thunder!' written on the board or on a large sheet of paper, photocopiable page 116.

What to do
This is a simple idea that allows the children to make full use of their imagination and at the same time work within a tight structure. It also gives you the opportunity to discuss some excellent teaching points about how the poem is set out and written.

Read the following poem to the children:

Louder than a clap of thunder!

Louder than a clap of thunder,
louder than an eagle screams,
louder than a dragon blunders,
or a dozen football teams,
louder than a four-alarmer,
or a rushing waterfall,
louder than a knight in armor
jumping from a ten-foot wall.

Louder than an earthquake rumbles,
louder than a tidal wave,
louder than an ogre grumbles
as he stumbles through his cave,
louder than stampeding cattle,
louder than a cannon roars,
louder than a giant's rattle,
that's how loud my father SNORES!

Jack Prelutsky

Discuss the poem with the class and see if they have any further louder ideas. Use the first verse of the poem to bring out the following teaching points.

● How has the poet decided to set the poem out?
(Each idea is on a separate line apart from the description of the knight which has taken up two lines.)

● Has he put commas at the end of every line? If not then why not?
(He has put commas at the end of each separate idea but not at the end of the second last line because he is still describing the knight and this has carried onto the next line. As the description is still continuing, the poet has considered that a comma is not required.)

● The poet has used rhyme in the poem. Can you work out the pattern of rhyme he has employed?
(a, b, a, b,)

● Has he started each line with a capital letter? Why not?
(No he hasn't; basically the poet has the option whether to or not.)

● Has he started each line with 'louder than . . .'?
(Definitely not!)

● Do you think it would have been better if he had done? Try reading the verse with every line starting with 'louder than'.
(By varying the beginning it makes the poem more interesting and easier to read aloud.)

● What other idea or emotion do you think he could have used?
(Quieter, softer, tougher, sillier, funnier, scarier, wetter, harder, faster, angrier, slower, more boring, more careless, more forgetful and so on.)

The children can now be asked to write their own poems using a different idea. However, before they start, the whole poem should be read again and this time the ending should be pointed out to the children. They can then be challenged to see if they can come up with one as amusing or as thoughtful for their own poems. Obviously the success of this and the length of the poem will depend on the children's age and ability. If you wanted the children to try rhyme they could have fun with the rhyme wheel on photocopiable page 116.

Haiku

Age range
Seven to eleven.

What to do
Haiku is a form of Japanese descriptive poetry that is normally concerned with nature. It follows a strict form consisting of three lines of five, then seven and then five syllables. Initially, when asking children to compose their own haiku, it is probably best to allow them some leeway. Ask them to write using the following guidelines:
● Use only three lines.
● Read your ideas over to yourself in your head.
● Start a new line when you pause.
● Where possible try and make your middle line the longest.
● Make sure you don't waste words – don't repeat the title in the poem.

Children enjoy writing haiku because of the brevity and simple formula. The best starting point is the season at hand. Discuss its characteristics and then ask the children to write a haiku on a specific topic such as sun, snow, leaves, wind and so on. Encourage the children to use all their senses to expand their feelings and experiences in their writing.

Christmas Eve

One single star,
a silver medal hanging
on an ebony neck.

Autumn trees

Proudly they stand;
upturned paint brushes
daubed in rustic hues.

Ask the children to use the same sort of structure to write their own poems about different everyday occurrences:
● getting up in the morning;
● having breakfast;
● going to school;
● bath time;
● following a recipe.

As in the example above, they can write one idea per line and then switch words between lines.

Nonsense

Age range
Seven to eleven.

What to do
Children find simple nonsense poetry good fun to read and write. The following poem 'I said my pyjamas' is a typical example of how to interchange one or two words, still retain meaning and create an enjoyable, humorous poem.

I said my pyjamas

I said my pyjamas
I put on my prayers,
I went up my slippers,
I took off my stairs,
I switched off the bed,
I jumped in the light,
The reason for this is,
You kissed me goodnight.

Anonymous

Shape poetry

Age range
Seven to eleven.

What you need
Photocopiable page 117.

What to do
Shape or concrete poetry is where poetic language is arranged in the shape of the subject of the poem.

The plant

```
        thirsty,      for
     always                a
  is                          fresh
     plant              rainy
        a      shower.
           flower,
            the
            to
            leaf,
            the
            to
            stem,
            the
            to
            root,
            the
            *From
```

A good way to get children started with this exercise is to use photocopiable page 117. The children should write the words of their poems round the shapes. They could then follow this up by inventing their own shape poems.

52

Excuses!

Age range
Seven to eleven.

What to do

Kidnapped!

This morning I got kidnapped
By three masked men.
They stopped me on the sidewalk,
And offered me some candy,
And when I wouldn't take it
They grabbed me by the collar,
And pinned my arms behind me,
And shoved me in the backseat
Of this big black limousine and
Tied my hands behind my back
With sharp and rusty wire.
Then they put a blindfold on me
So I couldn't see where they took me,
And plugged up my ears with cotton
So I couldn't hear their voices.
And drove me for 20 miles or
At least 20 minutes, and then
Dragged me from the car down to
Some cold and moldy basement,
Where they stuck me in a corner
And went off to get the ransom
Leaving one of them to guard me
With a shotgun pointed at me,
Tied up sitting on a stool . . .
That's why I'm late for school!

Shel Silverstein

Read this poem and sit back while the children have fun inventing their own excuses about being late for school. The challenge is now on for the children to write a poem about an extended excuse such as being involved in a robbery, meeting aliens, finding a time machine and so on. If they would rather, the children could make up a list poem of different excuses, for example, 'I couldn't get the toothpaste back in the tube, my alarm clock ran out of petrol . . .'.

53

What is . . . the sun?

The sun is an orange dinghy
   sailing across a calm sea.

It is a gold coin
   dropped down a drain in heaven.

It is a yellow beach ball
   kicked high into the summer sky.

It is a red thumb-print
   on a sheet of pale blue paper.

It is the gold top from a milk bottle
   floating on a puddle.

Wes Magee

Similes and metaphors

Age range
Seven to eleven.

What to do
Similes compare one thing to another and are
introduced by the words 'like' or 'as', for example, 'he
was *as* light as a feather' and 'she was *like* a human
dustbin'. They play a very important role in our writing
in allowing us to reinforce and clarify ideas. They also
afford the writer an imaginative way to entertain the
reader.

   Metaphors are very similar to similes but they are not
introduced by 'like' or 'as'. Metaphors can appear much
stronger and more direct than a simile. Both similes and
metaphors allow the writer to create helpful and
powerful imagery.

   Having explained to the children what similes and
metaphors are, read them the following poem.

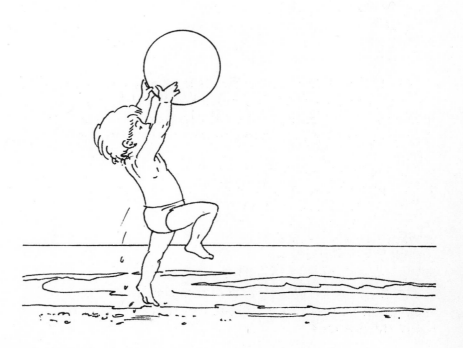

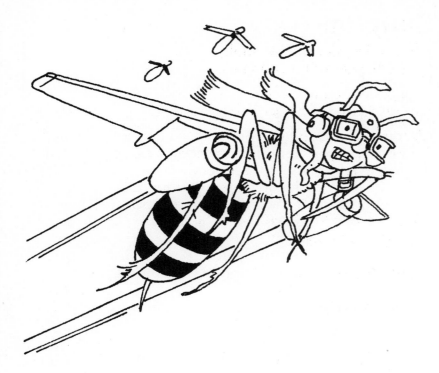

Talk to the children about well-known sayings such as 'as sharp as a needle' and ask them to think of some alternatives, for example, 'as sharp as a pencil point'.

Ask the children to write similes for the following topics:
- The wet mud was like . . .
- The moon hung in the sky like . . .
- The storm was as violent as . . .
- The leaves fell like . . .
- The fog arrived like a . . .
- The wind was like a . . .
- The tree waved as though it were . . .

Ask the children to read out their similes and then to read them as metaphors. Does the class notice any slight difference?

The children could now try and work on a poem using metaphors and similes. Ask them to think of an interesting creature and liken it to:
- a household object or machine;
- a type of weather or season;
- a type of person or another creature.

For example, if they chose a wasp then they might respond with:
- an aeroplane;
- autumn;
- an angry person.

They should then choose from this list the topic that they feel would be the most productive. In the case of the wasp it might be an aeroplane. They should then write about the creature as if they are this object.

Bombers!

Engines buzz,
wings flap,
as yellow aerodynamic bodies
hit the air.
Black insignia,
an omen to all
of a possible sting in the tail.
Venom tipped missiles
armed for launching.

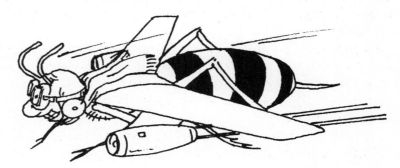

Couplets

Age range
Eight to eleven.

What to do
Couplets are two-lined verses which normally rhyme. Ezra Pound, an American poet, created a specific style of couplet which was subsequently named after him. The idea was to write the first line of the couplet as a description and the second as a metaphor. The two ideas are separated by a semi-colon.

The early morning sun;
An orange balloon waiting to be popped.

The smoke from a chimney;
A long grey scarf.

Ask the children to try writing their own Ezra Couplets. It is an excellent way of developing the appreciation of the metaphor and developing imagination.

Collective poems

Age range
Eight to eleven.

What to do
Collective nouns such as a *bunch* of grapes or a *flock* of birds are commonplace in everyday conversation.

Ask the children to write collective poems in which they devise their own collective nouns. This will help them to stretch their imagination and use originality. You could suggest that they make them alliterative.

Collection time

Yesterday I noticed,

a buzz of bees,
a chapter of books,
a cuddle of coats,
a team of footballs,
a bag of belly buttons,
a roof of houses,
a scribble of pens
and an exhaust of cars.

They were all cool, calm and collected!

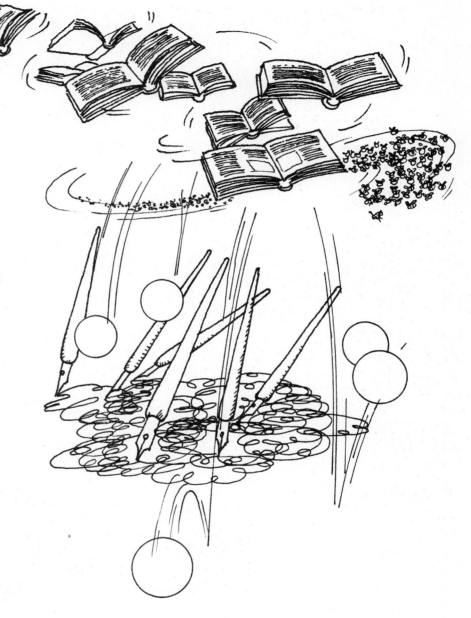

Happiness   Sadness
Friends School   Morning
Christmas

Definition poetry

Age range
Eight to eleven.

What to do
Definition poetry is when a specific topic is taken and defined in as many interesting ways as possible, for example:

What's night?

A dark ceiling,
a blackboard of sky,
a light-taker,
a shadow-maker,
an announcement of sleep,
a nightmare and dream time.

That's sleep!

Ask the children to write their own definition poems. Encourage them to think of clear, original imagery. By doing this they will be forced to concentrate hard on one particular topic and cover as many different aspects of it as they can.

A few of the many topics for scrutinising and defining are: anger, fear, storms, seasons, sports, poetry, friendship, books and teachers.

Diamante

Age range
Eight to eleven.

What to do
A diamante is interesting, thoughtful and fun to write.
The idea is to set a poem out so that it is in the shape of
a diamond. The poem starts at the top with the subject
and then moves down the shape to the bottom where it
finishes as an antonym.

Ask the children to write a diamante. They should
structure their poems as follows:
- topic (noun);
- two adjectives;
- three action words (-ing words);
- four nouns (two of which describe the topic and two
the antonym);
- three action words (-ing words);
- two adjectives;
- antonym (noun).

```
                    City
              busy,      noisy
       bustling,    sprawling,    polluting
   streets,    roads,    ———    fields,    lanes,
       farming,    flowering,    blossoming
              scenic,    tranquil
                  Countryside
```

Before the children attempt a diamante they need to
think of suitable opposites, such as night/day, winter/
summer, friend/enemy and so on. They will find a
thesaurus a great help when doing this.

59

Limericks

Age range
Eight to eleven.

What you need
Photocopiable page 116.

What to do
Limericks are humorous poems which were popularised in the nineteenth century by Edward Lear. They consist of five lines, with lines three and four being shorter in length, and follow a set rhyming pattern (a, a, b, b, a); for example:

A teacher from Harrow

There was a young teacher from Harrow
Whose nose was too long and too narrow.
It gave so much trouble
That he bent it double
And wheeled it round school in a barrow.

Anonymous

Ask the children to write their own limericks. However, before you let them tackle their limericks, it is a good idea to try writing one as a whole class. This hopefully allows everyone to concentrate on the teaching points as well as be aware of the rhyming patterns. The communal sharing of the writing difficulties is of great benefit to all. Possible first lines are:
- There was a young girl called Nelly;
- There was a young fellow called Guy;
- A policeman out on the beat;
- One night as Dan went to bed.

The rhyme wheel on photocopiable page 116 should be helpful when writing this type of poetry.

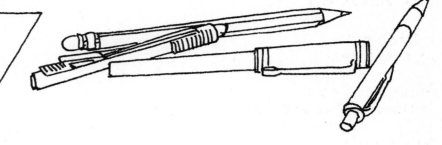

What am I?
A way of speaking without seeing
Press me if modern
The long way if not
I'm great for pizza
Or even the weather
If you're far away
I'll keep you together.

Answer: Telephone

Riddles

Age range
Eight to eleven.

What to do
Riddle poems are basically word puzzles. Children find them thoughtful and challenging to write and fun to solve.

Ask the children to choose a subject, for example, a washing machine, spider, butterfly and so on. Then, tell them to write a rough description of the object: what it looks like, what it does, what it reminds them of and so on.

Once they have noted down their rough description, tell the children to use their notes to write their riddle. Remind them that they must not mention their subject in the poem or title! And remind them that it doesn't have to rhyme.

Riddle

A word collection
for
meaning detection.

A fact-finder
and
spelling reminder.

A language arranger
also
information exchanger.

A knowledge hoarder
in
alphabetical order.

(Answer: a dictionary)

Follow-up
The children may like to write a riddle about someone in the school. After they have written down the basics ask them to add one or two similes or metaphors concerning their chosen person. Once they are finished, all the poems can be read out to the rest of the class who then have to try and guess who they are.

Very, very strict!

Age range
Eight to eleven.

What to do

Oliver's parents in the morning

Oliver's parents are very, very strict. This is how strict they are in the morning.

1. When Oliver's radio alarm goes off, Oliver's parents say, 'Oliver, turn that rock music up as loud as it will go so it wakes the whole neighbourhood! Otherwise, we will be very upset with you!'

2. At breakfast Oliver's parents say, 'Oliver, you'd better make sure you spill at least half of those Sugar Crumblies on the floor, and don't you dare clean them up either!'

3. After breakfast Oliver's parents say, 'Oliver, you must get dressed very, very slowly so the school bus has to honk a lot while it's waiting for you. Otherwise, you will be in deep trouble.'
Oliver's parents are very, very strict. Aren't you glad they're not yours?

Jeff Moss

Read the poem 'Oliver's parents' to the children. They will probably hugely enjoy the inverted twist of the parents' responses. Discuss with them other home situations where parents might give an unexpected response; for example, tidying up the bedroom, putting away toys, coming to talk to visitors, helping to look after a baby brother or sister and so on. Ask the children to write their own versions of what their parents might say. They could use their own names as the central character.

This idea can be extended to other relations, clubs attended and responses by organisers as well as the school. Surprisingly enough the children really enjoy writing about their teachers!

Cinquain

Age range
Nine to eleven.

What to do
The cinquain is a poem which consists of five unrhymed lines with a formation of two, then four, six, eight and two syllables per line. However, a version of cinquain that is not quite so restricting and which may be easier for the children to write runs as follows:
- one noun (topic);
- two adjectives;
- three action words (-ing words);
- a feeling about it (four words);
- one synonym or strong expressive word related to the topic.

An example of such a poem is:

Space,
Mysterious, alien,
Absorbing, fascinating, challenging,
Stretching out into infinity,
Universal.

There are many topics that the children might consider, for example the playground, a famous person, a film, a sport or a hobby and so on.

Dada

Age range
Nine to eleven.

What to do
Dada poetry originated in Paris and was used by many poets and artists to write nonsense poems. The idea of this form of poetry is to make up or select:
- ten verbs;
- eight nouns;
- eight pronouns. (They don't all have to be used but they must use a minimum of six and if possible, all!)

Having chosen their words the children can write them out on small pieces of paper and then jumble them up and arrange them as they like.

> they sneeze a hiccup
> squeeze a dragon
> seize the she key
> chase the he cat
> eat her tree wheel
> shout gun fall

The children might like to ask a friend to organise their words. They can make this really difficult if they like by giving one word a capital letter and another a full stop so that there is no choice about which words are used to start and finish the poem.

AacHOOo!

Found poetry

Age range
Nine to eleven.

What you need
Magazines, newspapers, advertisements.

What to do
Found poetry is where ideas and words are taken from newspaper articles, magazines and advertisements and reworked as poems. Found poems allow children to concentrate on the pattern and rhythm of a poem, as the subject and a lot of the words are already provided for them. When you display the children's poems it is interesting to have the original article placed next to them for all to compare and consider.

Found poems can also be used to highlight certain aspects of the media and advertising. The following poem shows the style and hype that advertisers often use to sell. The product discussed is actually a watch which has a blood pressure check.

Extract from an advert for . . .?

The BP100
can monitor your pulse and blood pressure,
both Systolic and Diastolic,
at the touch of a button.

In memory mode,
30 readings can be stored,
giving you the time
and date of the check
allowing you to review progress.

In Bioflashback mode,
target rates are stored,
allowing you to compare actual readings
against your targets.
Useful for anyone
perfecting relaxation techniques
or trying to control blood pressure.

But that's not all!

The actual wording in the advertisement was as follows:
'Because the BP100 can monitor your pulse and blood pressure, both Systolic and Diastolic, at the touch of a button.

In memory mode, up to 30 readings can be stored giving you the time and date of the check allowing you to review your progress.

In Bioflashback mode, target rates are stored allowing you to compare actual readings against your targets. Useful for anyone perfecting their relaxation techniques or simply trying to control their blood pressure.'

Hyperbole

Age range
Nine to eleven.

What to do
Hyperbole is a style of writing where exaggeration is used to create and emphasise a particular point, for example, 'He was built like the side of a house' or 'She spends money like water'. It is also a form of writing which helps children to develop vivid descriptions and extend their imagination.

Ask the children to answer the following questions and remember to stress they must try to exaggerate.
● How angry was the man?
Answer: He was an erupting volcano.

● How fast was the sports car?
● How dark was it?
● How loud was the music?
● How tall was his father?
● How wet did she get?
● How cold was the water?
● How thin was he?

The children can obviously make up their own sentences if they wish and then read them out and compare them with the rest of the class.

Once the children have made up their sentences they can attempt to write their own poems around subjects that allow for exaggeration, for example:
● If you were the richest school child in the world . . .
● If you were the cleverest person in the world . . .
● You have just become aware that you have an incredible special power.

Personification

Age range
Nine to eleven.

What to do
When we give human characteristics to everyday things, ideas, objects and animals this is called personification. Personification can be a powerful, original and very effective style of writing but it is probably best tackled by the upper juniors. The idea, as with many in the book, can obviously carry over into the children's writing of prose.

Read the children the following poem. (It would help if the children had a copy of the poem or it was written on the board.)

The early morning

The early morning
exhales a cool breath
over the lifeless, languid trees.
Gradually,
they stretch themselves awake
and rhythmically begin
exercising their taut, brown limbs.

Once you have read the poem through a couple of times you can discuss with the children:
● the structure of the poem;
● what they liked and did not like about the poem;
● the parts in the poem that were personified;
● how else the early morning and the trees could be personified.

The children can then attempt to write their own poems using personification. Their poems need only be a short description but they should be as thoughtful and original as possible. They could write about such things as a storm, fog, night, rain or fire and so on.

Follow-up
Give the children a statement and then ask them to respond to a set question in a personified form, for example:
● I remember when we moved house. How did the house feel about it?
● Last night there was a terrible storm. How did the storm feel? Was it upset or enjoying itself?
● The car, which had not been used for a week, would not start. How did it feel? Why wouldn't it start?
● The television set was left on in the front room with no one listening. How does it feel at being ignored?
● The old train was late and suddenly it had to race along to catch up. How does it feel being treated in this way, particularly at its time of life?
● The leaf turned from green to brown and was discarded by its tree. How does it feel as it floats to the ground?

Poetry and prose

Age range
Nine to eleven.

What to do
Read the following pieces of prose and poetry to the children. It would be best if you could write both versions on the board.

A seashore breakfast

Early one morning I watch the sea. It appears to be breakfasting; chewing on the seashore with its sharp teeth of white waves. It seems to me that it is biting deeply into crunchy, rock pools and lapping up a cereal of golden, brown sand. Then occasionally I see it spit out the bits that are inedible; the pollution of human left overs. Finally, it appears to have had enough and licking its salty lips it slides back down the shore. Before it goes I think I hear it announce that it will be back later for more.

A seashore breakfast

Early morning,
and the sea is breakfasting;
Chewing hungrily on the seashore
With its sharp teeth of white waves.
Biting deeply into crunchy rock pools
and lapping up a cereal of golden
brown sand.

Occasionally it spits the bits that are inedible.
The pollution of human left overs.
Until finally, it licks its salty lips
and slides back down the shore,
Shouting, 'I'll be back later, for more!'

Discuss the two pieces with the children highlighting the obvious differences between the poem and the piece of prose. Does one create a clearer meaning than the other? Which one has more impact and why? How would they have set the poem out?

Now ask the children to try altering the following piece of prose into a poetic form.

The Storm

This morning, because a storm was hustling across the sky, it reminded me of a dark sheet of paper. It really looked like it meant business because it was full of black lumps of cloud looking for trouble. Before long the sky had changed into a dirty dishcloth that rinsed itself all over and around our street.

Finally, ask the children to write a piece of prose on a selected topic of their choice and then rewrite it as a poem.

Poetry styles

Age range
Nine to eleven.

What you need
Photocopiable page 118 and 119.

What to do
This activity helps to reinforce children's awareness of all the various styles and forms within poetry. Photocopiable pages 118 and 119 showing different forms of poetry could be used prior to this activity.

Read out several simple poems that have been written in different poetic styles and forms and are not known by the children. Read them one at a time without letting the children see any of the poems, just listening. Ask them to write out each poem in the format they feel the poet might have used.

It will depend on the children as to how much help you give them, but when there is clearly a pause in the reading a new line should be started. The children will enjoy comparing their efforts with the original.

Questions and answers

Age range
Nine to eleven.

Group size
Pairs.

What to do
Children have a tremendous thirst for knowledge and are continually questioning and querying the world around them. This activity allows them to ask their questions and hopefully get an imaginative response.

Ask the children to think of and write down a list of five or six questions. They should be relatively thoughtful, for example, 'Why is the earth round? Why is snow white?' When they have finished writing their questions they should exchange books with a friend and begin using their imaginations to respond to the questions set by their partner.

They could just end up with a poem to read out to the class!

Questions and answers

Why is there an R in Rodney's name?
Because if there wasn't he would be called Odney!
Why have we got names and not numbers?
Would you want to be called 12,473¼?
Why do we have such funny arms?
So we can blow our runny noses.
Why do we have a belly button?
Because it's less painful than a belly zip.
Why do some trees grow so tall?
Because they eat too much.
Why are boxes square?
If they were round they'd all roll away.
Why do we have radiators?
Because teleators would need aerials.
And finally where does the sea start?
At the beginning of course!

Thin poems

Age range
Nine to eleven.

What to do
Thin poems, as the name suggests, are poems that are written in a narrow, elongated shape. They are rhythmic poems written in a, a, b, b rhyme and usually contain lines of no more than two or three syllables as with the following poem 'Summer fun'.

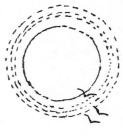

Summer fun

Sunshine,
All's fine.
In car,
Not far.
Park, ride,
Seaside.
On sand,
As planned.
Deckchair,
Take care.
Swim wear,
Somewhere.
Don't howl,
Found towel.
Beach clad,
Even Dad.
Beach swim,
Water skim.
One splash,
All dash.
One shout,
All out.
Soaking wet,
No regret.
Water salty,

NOT
My faulty.
Awful thirst,
Drink first.
Beach flop,
Lollipop.
Hot feet,
Lunch eat.
Mum burns,
Body turns.
Dad snores,
BOTH BORES!
Sand play,
HOORAY!
Real hassle,
Sand castle.
Bat, ball,
Sister call.
Run, catch,
No match.
Getting late,
Bus wait.
Goodbye,
Sea, sky.
SUMMER FUN,
NUMBER ONE!

72

Apart from helping to teach syllable counts, writing thin poems is an ideal way for writing up-tempo poems with plenty of action. This of course makes them great fun for performing to an audience in assemblies, plays, and to other classes. Other possible subjects are machines, storms, raps and in particular different forms of sport such as athletics, football, netball, rounders and cricket.

Topical poetry

Hands

Age range
Five to eight.

What to do

Hands

My hands
can
scratch and catch,
can
climb and mime,
can
crack and whack,
can
bleed and lead,
can
pick and click,
can
wave and misbehave,
can
break and ache
and even shake
each other by the hand.
My hands — such hand-dandy friends!

Read the above poem to the children and then ask them to talk about what their hands can do. Ask them to think about what their hands remind them of and discuss with them what their hands look like. Having discussed their hands the children can make a detailed sketch of them, showing lines, scars, wrinkles and all.

Read the poem again or any other suitable hand poems that you may know. Tell the children to make up their own poems starting with the line 'My hands can . . .' Do they think their hands change with their emotions, for example when they are happy, angry or frightened?

Body parts

Age range
Five to nine.

What you need
A thesaurus.

What to do
This is an excellent way to develop the children's vocabulary and use of the thesaurus. Ask the children to draw round their own hands or feet and then begin to write all the various verbs relating to hands or feet inside their sketch. Older children can be encouraged to find words in a thesaurus.

With young children it is best to ask them what their own hands or feet are able to do. You can often widen the vocabulary by suggesting they think of other people of different ages such as their mothers, fathers or grandparents.

Later, the children can, of course, attempt the same idea with different body parts such as the heart, nose, ear, finger, eye and so on. They will have to make their own sketch of these body parts, so the size and scale they choose will be important.

Creepy-crawly creatures

Age range
Five to eleven.

What you need
Magnifying glasses, rubber gloves.

What to do
The study of spiders, centipedes, ants, worms, caterpillars and other such creatures can make a fascinating topic to inspire the children to write. It is also an ideal topic for firsthand observation and sensory work.

In order to inspire children try to visit a nearby wood or conservation area where they can see minibeasts in their natural habitat. Discuss with the children what sort of creatures live in the earth and ask them to tell you any unusual or amusing incidents about them.

Let the children examine some soil. (The children should wear rubber gloves.) What sort of texture does it have? Is it damp, dry or loose? Are there any living creatures in it? If so, how do they move? Have magnifying glasses available for close observation.

You might also like to set up a wormery in the classroom. The children will then be able to look at the colour, shape and length of worms and if they are careful, they can also handle them.

The children might also do some further research about minibeasts in a suitable place in the school grounds or if this is not possible from books in the library. They could use a recording sheet to write down their facts or any ideas gathered. (If the children are working with minibeasts they should handle them with care and return them to their habitat once the work is completed.)

Now that the children know a little bit more about minibeasts you could read them the following poem.

My garden wall

Beside my garden wall,
Live creatures great and small.

Inside deep, dark places,
You'll find centipedes with puzzled faces,
Counting feet for evermore,
And each time there seems to be just two more!

Stitched carefully on to leafy stems,
You can discover ladybird button gems.
But be told and beware of this attractive sight,
For when annoyed they really do bite!

Half-way up the garden wall,
Trying hard not to slip or fall,
Spider is pretending to draw a silky map,
But in fact it is a sticky, insect trap!

While quietly underneath and underground,
Earthworms chew busily, not making a sound.
Then off they squirm for all their worth,
Like farmers ploughing the rich brown earth.

A butterfly occasionally dances into sight,
Floating like a coloured kite.
Fluttering high, fluttering low,
Searching nectar to help it grow.

And today perched carefully on top of my garden wall,
Sits mother sun watching warmly over them all.

Discuss with the children:
- which description of a creature did they enjoy?
- if they were to add another verse what would it say?
- what are their own gardens like?
- for those without a garden how do they feel?
- do they have a balcony, flower boxes or a park nearby?

The children should now, hopefully, have enough information and be at a stage where they could write their own poems on minibeasts.

Colours

Age range
Five to eleven.

What to do
Colour is a popular topic to use with young children. The following is a simple idea for a list poem that will interest and allow the children to think about colour.

Read the poem 'Green' to the children and then discuss with them what their favourite colours are and, where possible, why.

Green!

Green is the park nearby;
it is my best sweatshirt.

Green is a Christmas tree;
it is my school sandwich box.

Green is my favourite lime drink;
it is the pattern on my wallpaper.

Green is a spring morning;
it is fresh and bouncy.

But guess what?
Red's the best!

Ask the children to write their own colour poems based on the format of the above poem. To avoid the monotony of repeating the lines 'Green is . . .' on every single line it could be suggested that the children follow the pattern or similar one to that of the poem.

Once the poems have been completed they can be written out in best and decorated with pictures and paintings.

You could use a more thoughtful approach with older children. Ask them to consider what a colour reminds or makes them think of, rather than what the colour actually represents, for example:

Black

Shadows crawling across my garden;
darkness following me upstairs.
The cold breath of night;
silence wrapping itself around me.

When writing this type of poem tell the children only to refer to the colour in the title or use it very sparingly throughout the poem.

Fruit fun!

Age range
Six to nine.

Group size
Small groups.

What you need
Fruit, magnifying glasses, a knife.

What to do
This activity can be used as a way of developing the children's senses. Give each group a piece of fruit, either all the same type or a selection of apples, bananas, oranges and so on. Ask the children to look closely at the fruit. First they should look at them with a magnifying glass and then use their senses of sight, touch and smell.

Having done this, you can peel or cut the fruit and allow the children to eat a small piece. (NB: It is important to be aware of any food allergies which children may have.) The class can now respond to the following questions.
● What did your piece of fruit look like?
● How did I feel?
● What did it smell like?
● How did it feel when you bit into it?
● Describe how it tasted when you swallowed it.
Ask the children to précis their answers to the first four questions into one word and then one sentence for the last question. They can then use these as a poem.

My orange

Bumpy,
shiny,
juicy,
delicious.
My mouth wants more!

Days of the week

Age range
Six to nine.

What to do
The days of the week can offer a suitable structure around which the children can construct a poem. The following poem uses the idea of 'the terrible week'. Read it to the children and ask them to write their own poem about an exciting/boring/funny/unusual/fantastical or indeed, as in the poem, a horrid week.

Germs

On Monday I caught
Measles, mumps and malaria
And I meandered home.

On Tuesday I caught
Typhoid, tummy ache and TB
And I tumbled home.

On Wednesday I caught
Worms, warts and wet the bed
And I wobbled home.

On Thursday I caught
A sore throat, tonsillitis and broke three fingers
And I tripped home.

On Friday I caught
a fever, flu and fleas
And fell all the way home.

On Saturday I caught
Shingles, spots and was sick
And I shuddered home.

On Sunday I caught
Smallpox, sneezes and sores
And I stayed in bed.

Anonymous

Friendship is . . .

Age range
Six to nine.

What to do
Let the children use the simple structure of the poem below to write their own poems. They can use various themes including sadness, happiness, being fed up, excitement, fear, anger and so on.

> Friendship is sharing secrets.
> It is laughing and joking.
> Friendship is someone always there.
> It is caring.
> Friendship is saying sorry.
> It is just being together.
> Friendship is a warm feeling.

When working with slightly older children you can read them the poem 'Friends'. If possible they should each have a copy of the poem.

Friends

As friends we
whisper,
discuss,
argue,
then float messages across crowded playgrounds
that only we know and understand.

As friends we
walk,
stumble,
run,
then sprint after each other,
so close we exchange shadows as we go.

As friends we
laugh,
cry,
care,
taste each others thoughts
and share each others moods.

One girl, one boy,
one friendship to enjoy.
One lock, one key
that's you and me!

Discuss with the children:
- what repeating pattern they can see with the first three verses;
- why they think the verses were set out in this way;
- which parts in the poem they enjoyed;
- what sorts of things they get up to with their friends in the playground;
- whether they prefer to have one particular friend or many.

   Having discussed the poem ask the children to write a poem on one of the following topics:
- What do you think makes a good friend?
- What is the best thing a friend has ever done for you?
- How do you go about making a friend?
- How do you feel when you fall out with a friend?
- Why are friends so important?
- How do you feel about sharing your friends?

   They should consider whether to write about one friend in particular or friends in general, and also whether or not they are going to make their poems rhyme.

Magic shoes

Age range
Six to nine.

What to do
We have all dreamed of the idea of being granted wishes whether it's by a good fairy or a genie, the excuse to daydream of wondrous wealth or doing the impossible lies within us all.

   Before reading the poem 'Magic shoes', discuss with the children their favourite wishes and what might develop if they were granted three wishes.

Magic shoes

I've got a pair of magic shoes
they take me to the moon.
Dad says, 'Watch out for the rockets,'
and Mum says, 'Come back soon.'

I've got a pair of magic shoes
they take me to the stars,
and sometimes if I'm early,
I'll stop for tea on Mars.

I've got a pair of magic shoes
I can jump as high as a school,
I can walk up walls like Spiderman
and act like I'm really cool.

I've got a pair of magic shoes
I can dance like a disco king,
they spring me up to the rooftops,
they let me do anything.

But what if I had some magic socks,
some magic underwear too!
with a magic suit of clothes
there's nothing I couldn't do.

Brian Moses

A reading of 'Magic shoes' will confine the subject area to physical activities and what the children would do with their own pair of 'magic shoes'. The children could then write about their own adventures either with 'magic shoes' or some other magical article such as a coat, gloves, scarf, glasses, bicycle and so on. This might also lend itself to some amusing and imaginative art work.

It would be helpful, particularly with young children, to discuss the rhyming patterns within the poem and perhaps give them the first two lines:

I've got a pair of magic shoes
they take me to the moon (outer space, the shops, into town, through the air, into my dreams)

Sensible poems

Age range
Six to nine.

What you need
Photocopiable page 120, dictionaries, thesauruses.

What to do
Give each child a copy of photocopiable page 120 and ask them to complete each category. This will help build up their vocabulary knowledge and become more familiar with a thesaurus. Two examples in each section have been given.

Having completed photocopiable page 120 the children need to choose a topic to write about in which they can include most or all of their senses. Food is a good subject when writing using the senses and a poem could be written about a particular meal such as Christmas dinner or Sunday lunch.

The SENSEble Sunday Lunch

I SMELL the roast beef
as it sizzles and splutters in the oven.

I TASTE the finger-licking Yorkshire pudding
that hides inside a bowl.

I SEE Mum flying round the kitchen
like a busy buzzy bee.

I HEAR Dad snoring at the television
while it tries to wake him up.

I FEEL Mr Hungry on the prowl
as it growls inside my stomach.

But suddenly his waiting is at an end.
The Sunday roast is finally ready!

The children could use another structure for sensory writing by writing three or four lines around specific senses, for example:

I wish

I wish I could:
See my bedroom full of new toys,
See a library of my favourite authors,
See the beach from last year's holiday,
And see my gran more often.

The poem would continue in a similar way but using 'I wish I could taste/hear/smell/touch'.

If the children write poems using this idea, then remind them not to place an idea in the wrong section, for example, don't write 'see my favourite meal' when that obviously would be better in the taste section!

Pets

Age range
Six to eleven.

What to do
Most children own or have owned or know someone who has a pet. From dogs, cats through to hamsters, budgies, rabbits and goldfish, pets have their say in most households. This means that children are able to write from firsthand experience about pets. Before you ask the children to write their poems, it is a good idea to let them have time to observe their pets and, if appropriate, take notes.

When they come to write their poems, give the children the following succinct structure to work to.
● animal – cat,
● describe it – black and sleek,
● how does it move? – melts inside the shadows,
● does it make a noise? – on silent paws,
● where is it going/coming from? – searching a midday meal,
● last line/summary – satisfied it pads off purring.

Discuss this structure and let the children write their poems. Ask the children to read their poems to the rest of the class and then move on to try and develop a longer, more thoughtful piece of writing using the following questions.
● Can you describe your pet?
● What does your pet like and dislike?
● Does your pet have any funny, peculiar or annoying habits?
● How does it behave near other animals?
● How do you know when it is happy, fed up or hungry?
● Has it got a favourite place in the house?

● What does it enjoy doing most, for example, eating, sleeping, getting up to mischief?

If they so wish the children can write about a completely new pet or carry forward their initial ideas.

Read to the children the poem 'Scat cat'.

Scat cat

Our cat,
skims across floors,
spins round corners
chasing its own elusive tail.
A blur of ebony fur.

Our cat, scats downstairs;
ripping patterns in our carpet
with its sewing needle claws,
then pitter pats innocently out of sight.

Our cat,
drags a feathered sack of bird
into the kitchen.
Then stalks the garden;
freezing everything that moves.

Our cat,
sleek, slimlined,
feeds with feline satisfaction.
Then stealthily, mysteriously,
melts inside the waiting shadows.

Ask the children the following questions:
● Did any particular part of the poem make the children think about their own cat or pet?
● Did it remind them of other pet incidents?
● Why do they think the cat is described as 'a blur of ebony fur'?
● In the last line it says that the cat 'melts inside the waiting darkness'. Do they think this is an interesting way to describe the cat disappearing?
● Can they think of their own last line?

My bedroom

Age range
Seven to eleven.

What to do
The day before you do this activity ask the children to take notes and if they wish, make a small sketch of their own bedrooms. Also go over the following questions with the children so that they will have some idea of what to take notes on.
● What shape is your bedroom?
● How is it decorated?
● How do you feel about your bedroom?
● What is the best and worst thing about your bedroom?
● How many windows have you in your bedroom?
● Describe the furniture.
● Do you share a bedroom? If so how do you feel about that?

● What can you hear from your bedroom at different times of the day?
● What would you most change about your bedroom?
   You might also like to read them Jamie Thomson's poem (see page 11).
● Is the description of Jamie's bedroom anything like their own?
● Do they think his bedroom sounds neat or untidy?
● Do they get into trouble for having an untidy room?
● What was Jamie's comparison in the poem?
● Do they have a cupboard or a perhaps a secret place in which they play or hide?
   Once the children have carried out their research they can begin to write their own poems. Remind them to consider the above questions as they draft their poems.
   Once the poems are all finished and neatly presented the children could add their own sketches.

Follow-up
Ask the children to write about and design their own 'perfect bedrooms'.

Buildings

Age range
Seven to eleven.

What to do
Take the children to look at some of the buildings in the
locality of the school. However, before you go make
sure that they have had a chance to look at their own
houses in detail first. On their return from the trip, talk
about the various types of buildings they have seen such
as shops, houses, cinemas, churches, stations and so on.
Discuss the children's own homes and whether they are
houses, flats, maisonettes, bungalows and so on. You
might also discuss the shapes and materials used in their
homes. Finally, having talked about different types of
buildings, ask the children to choose a particular shape
of building and to draw its outline. They can then write
their thoughts inside the building shape.

Read the children the poem called 'The deserted
house'. This works best with older children and if
possible they should have access to a copy of the poem.

The deserted house

The house is alone now
deserted of human life;
only the shadows can be seen
queuing up to get in.

A tattered silhouette
glued to a changing skyline,
it sits hunched up,
shoulders pulled in,
its grey roof bowed low
as if hiding some dark secret,
deep within.

The windows are all boarded or broken
but each time I pass
they seem to watch my every move.
And yesterday as I slipped by,
side-stepping the 'give-away crunch'
of those autumn leaves,
I noticed the front door lay half open,
inviting entry.

My eyes quickly stretched inside,
past the inhospitable welcome
of the house's front entrance
and into its sombre hallway.
There the air seemed to freeze
as the darkness appeared to have squeezed
into every possible corner
where it sat brooding.

But suddenly my eyes and thoughts
were forced back out of the house.
My stomach had tied itself into a knot!
A shadow had appeared,
a black outline had smeared
across a broken window pane.

The knot in my stomach jerked tighter
as the shadow grew a tail and head.
But as swiftly, deftly as we had arrived
we both disappeared together.
Perhaps the house wasn't so alone.
Perhaps its shadows had found themselves a
playmate!

Discuss with the children:
- whether they could picture the house in their minds?
- which parts of the poem helped them do this the most?
- do they know of a similar building?
- what does it mean when the poem mentions 'A tattered silhouette glued to a changing skyline'?
- what were their thoughts when the shadow grew a tail and a head?
- what or whom did they think the playmate was?

The house is given human characteristics. It 'sits hunched up, shoulders pulled in'. Ask the children to use this idea of a building having human characteristics in their own writing and to write a poem about a specific building. Is it deserted, noisy or unusual in some way? Where is it situated? Who lives in the building? What lies around the house?

Christmas is . . .

Age range
Seven to eleven.

What to do
Christmas is obviously a special time of year and it is lovely to read a variety of children's Christmas poems discussing the atmosphere and excitement of Christmas.

Read 'Our family Christmas' to the children and discuss it with them. Then ask the children to write their own 'Our/my family Christmas' from their family's point of view. Hopefully, they might include a 'Christmas for me is . . .' verse. If required, the structure shown in the poem could be written on the board and offered as a skeleton for those who might want to use it.

Our family Christmas

Christmas for my mum is . . .

staggering with Christmas shopping,
wrestling with Christmas presents
and sweltering over Christmas cooking
until she begins to resemble the Christmas turkey.
Red, hot and bothered.

Christmas for my dad is . . .

struggling with the Christmas tree,
muddling with the Christmas lights
and falling off the ladder twice
until eventually he can be found
resting his eyes on the sofa.
We don't know which to plug in –
dad or the lights!

Christmas for my sister is . . .

excitement crackling in her eyes
as she waits for presents to arrive.
Helping dad with the decorations,
some of which are made of chocolate.
Every time he turns round
somehow another one just disappears!

Christmas for our dog is . . .

simple!
she can't believe her luck.
THERE'S A TREE IN THE FRONT ROOM!
And the odd pink bauble hanging from it
which she loves to crunch.

Christmas for our family is . . .

Christmas Day finally arriving
along with Grandma and Grandad.
One great big parcel of
excitement, fun and warmth
which we all in our own way enjoy unwrapping.

The children could also try writing a Christmas acrostic. Remind them of the need for continuity, as often they will tend to run through Christmas Day in their poem until they get to the final 's' when they jump back to Christmas Eve with **S**anta arriving laden with presents!

Christmas

Cards snowing through our letterbox,
Holly and mistletoe decorate the house,
Red cheeks glisten in the frosty air,
Icicles hang like sharpened teeth,
Stockings open mouthed, wait to be filled,
Tuneful carols drift through the night air,
Mincemeat, turkey flavour the kitchen,
Assorted presents prop up the tree,
Shouts of joy, the first present, Christmas Day begins.

Family

Age range
Seven to eleven.

What to do
Ask the children to think of their family, relations, friends or pets in the form of metaphors. The poem 'In our family' provides a clear example and the children can use the structure of the poem if necessary.

In our family

In our family

Dad is three Shredded Wheat,
he's a faded pair of jeans,
he's a winning goal of football
and he's the thunder and lightning in a storm.

In our family,

Mum is a tumbling washing machine,
she's the crunch in autumn leaves,
she's the warmth inside my duvet
and she's the 'no' that you wish was a 'yes'.

In our family

Sam is a muddy wellington boot,
he's a lumpy plate of mashed potato,
he's porridge flying across the table
and he's the laughter in a game of hide and seek.

In our family

that leaves me!
And I'm . . .
NOT TELLING!

Machines

Age range
Seven to eleven.

What to do
The following poem has a strong rhythm, rhyme and alliteration. It can be read to the class or the class can recite it. If doing the latter, the class can be split into groups and the poem recited as an all-action human machine.

Machines

Munch, crunch, clickety, clackety,
Whirr, churr, bong, bang.
Grrr, whishity, zip, zap,
Whoosh, whish, whine, clang!

Machines, machines, machines, machines,
Everywhere, everywhere, even in dreams.
Clanging, banging, whirring and gurring,
Crashing, thrashing, cracking and whacking.
On roadways and railways,
On seaways and airways.
All we can see are machines, machines.
The world is metal and plastic it seems.

Machine, machine, machine, machine,
Everyone uses one even the Queen.
Washing, cooking, cleaning and preening,
Digging, jigging, repairing and blaring.
Stereo, washing machine, car, bus
Soon there'll be no need for any of US!

Encourage the children to write their own poems about machines, or indeed about an individual machine, such as a bulldozer, car, crane, bicycle or any household appliance. The following questions may help to give the children guidance in their writing:
● What size, shape and colour is your machine?
● What type of noise does it make?
● What does your machine do?
● Does it remind you of anything?
● What is it made of?
● What do you like or dislike about the machine?

Night

Age range
Seven to eleven.

What to do
Talk with the children about the night. How does
everything change at night (sun setting, shadows,
moonlight)? How does their bedroom change when the
light goes out? Are there any particular shapes or areas
of their room that worries them when the light goes out?
How do the sounds at night differ from during the rest of
the day? What about specific sounds they can hear
while lying in bed such as the television, clock, water
pipes, people talking and so on? Have any funny
unusual incidents occurred to them at night?

   After the discussion read the poem 'At night' to the
children.

At night

At night,
when out slips the light,
my room becomes a cage.
A black box of uneasy darkness,
until a rushing car,
splashes white light
like thinned paint across the far wall.

It's then I know,
it's then I see,
it's then I am
not alone!

For fear bubbles under my skin,
grips my body,
twists my stomach,
feeds on my frightened mind.

And shadows,
they wait to throw themselves over me!

   Discuss with the children:
● which part of the poem they found the most
interesting.
● did it make them think of their own bedroom at night?
Why?
● do they have any shadows, lights, sounds that
regularly come into their bedroom at night?
● in the poem the room becomes a cage and what other
comparison is made?
● does any of their furniture or clothes take on another
shape in the darkness?
● can they compare darkness itself to a creature or
piece of clothing, for example a black cape thrown over
the earth?

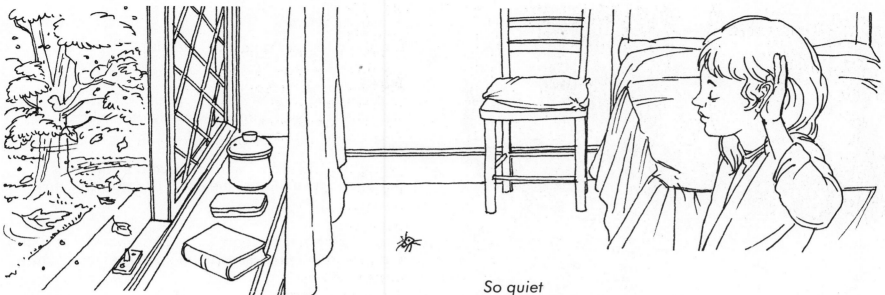

Quiet!

Age range
Seven to eleven.

What to do
As a poet you not only have to keep your eyes open but
your ears as well. Ask the children to sit in silence for
one minute and listen for all the noise going on in
school. Then, explain that you want them to use their
imagination and pretend that their ears have become
extra sensitive – in fact so sensitive that they can hear
sounds they could not hear before. It is a good idea to
have warned the children about the lesson beforehand
so that they can listen at home in various places for
unusual noises and to think about what or who might be
making the noise.

So quiet

One day it was so quiet
I could hear:
autumn leaves
parachuting on to the pavement.
A spider
crossing my bedroom carpet.
The garden tree
breathing in and out.
And the sun
melting in the sky.

Ask the children to try and write their own 'quiet'
poem. You might like to discuss with them where they
might be situated, for example in the town, home,
countryside, seaside, school and so on.

Follow-up
See the activity on 'Sounds' (page 98) for further ideas
on developing listening skills.

Seasons

Age range
Seven to eleven.

What to do
The seasons and the inevitable changes in weather, nature and our life-styles have always been an evocative and popular area for writers. The following ideas use autumn as their season but obviously any season can be treated in a similar fashion.

Initially read the following poem 'A taste of autumn' to the children. (It would be of help if the children had a copy to read as well.) Vivaldi's 'Autumn' from *The Four Seasons* could also be used to conjure up further autumnal images.

A taste of autumn

There is a taste of autumn in the air:

When,
an orange balloon of a sun pops up
and pats you NOT quite so warmly on the back.

When,
trees glow and show their newly coloured leaves
then spend them across the earth like golden coins.

When,
fruits and berries become early Christmas decorations
and mushroom umbrellas open up across the country fields.

When,
animals go eagerly shopping for their winter food
while swallows and martins sail south in search of warmth.

When,
flowers fold away their summer colours
and earlier than usual, the day runs out of light.

Freshly made and full of flavour,
autumn's a season I like to savour.

Having discussed the poem the children can have a go at writing their own poems. Provide the following questions to help stimulate their ideas.
- How do they know when autumn has arrived?
- How do some trees look as they lose their leaves?
- What is the difference between a deciduous tree and one that is evergreen?
- What is the best part of autumn?
- Can they think of any suitable similes for autumn?
- Some animals hibernate in autumn. Does their life-style change because of autumn? Think of weather and clothes and availability of food.
- If autumn was a person how would they describe it?

Once you have read the poem ask the children the following questions:
- Which parts did they enjoy?
- Were there descriptions or areas that they feel could have been better?
- What did the poem mean when it said 'the sun pops up and pats you NOT quite so warmly on the back' and 'flowers fold away their summer colours'?
- Are there any other areas of autumn that the poet could have mentioned?
- How many similes or metaphors did the poet use and what were they?

Sounds

Age range
Seven to eleven.

What you need
Tape recorder (optional).

What to do
Ask the children to make a list of sounds they can hear inside the school. Let them visit two or three different places with notepads or rough books. One or two children could take a tape recorder and record what they hear. This could then be played back and discussed at a later stage.

Ask the children to do the same thing standing outside in the playground and other suitable areas of the school. When the class is back in the classroom again discuss the various sounds they heard and see if the children can attribute a comparison/simile to them; for example, the secretary's telephone rang like a warning alarm.

Ask the children to write a sound poem. If you wish they can set it out as a simple comparing list poem, for example:

Inside school today I heard:

_____

_____

Outside school today I heard:

_____

_____

The poem 'The listening game' can be read to the children at whatever stage is thought best.

The listening game

In my room
I'm reading.
Eyes sucking at words
as though they are favourite sweets,
until I'm lost inside my book world.

Some twenty pages later,
to rest my eyes
and test my ears,
I play the listening game.

Downstairs Dad's voice is happily singing,
accompanied by water chuckling into the kitchen sink
and soon plates, dishes and cups
are setting sail across a bowl of bubbled foam.

Suddenly my baby sister
is pretending to be a police siren.
DAD-DEE! DAD-DEE! DAD-DEE! DAD-DEE!
but her voice quickly screeches to a halt
as she spots a new target,
DOG-GEE! DOG-GEE! DOG-GEE! DOG-GEE!

Meanwhile in the front room
all alone,
the television chats excitedly to itself
as it waits for an audience to arrive.

Some time later,
the house has yawned
and slowly drifted off to sleep.
Everything is
silent,
still,
frozen,
apart from the lick-tick of my bedroom clock,
not hurrying
just taking its time.

Follow-up
Ask the children to write about the sounds in their own
homes. They should find various places to listen in and
at different times of the day if possible. It is best if they
can take notes rather than rely on their memories. Their
notes will then provide a starting point for their writing.

Storm

Age range
Seven to eleven.

What to do
It would be helpful if the children were able to experience a storm at first hand; however, this may not be possible and so the next best thing is to use a sound effects tape. If the children are able to experience a storm ask them what sort of different sounds they hear as the storm arrives. Tell them to listen to the sound of the wind from different places such as next to a window, through a door. How do the sounds change? How does the sound of rain vary depending on where it falls, for example, a window, on the roof? What type of sound do they think it would make as it lands on the playground or trees? Can they see anything happening to the trees, bushes and flowers? How does their shape change? Ask the children to describe the sky. You could discuss the cloud shapes and their colours. Are they moving quickly or slowly? They could use their imagination and say why they think they might be in a hurry, for example, late for a special occasion, chasing someone, and so on. Also ask the children what it is like walking in a strong wind. What does the wind try to do to them and their clothes? Do they prefer to be outside or safely inside on a stormy day?

Once you have discussed the storm with the children read them the following poem:

Stormy temper

Yesterday I woke
to find my bedroom window
shivering on the wall.
While outside,
as the rain clapped loudly,
cars sprayed their way along the street.

Yesterday I walked outside
and immediately the cold licked my face
with its frozen tongue,
while the wind pushed past
to chase litter down the street.
Behind me the garden fence
began break dancing over the grass
and the washing line skipped across a bruised sky.

Yesterday I watched,
as the weather got really angry
and ripped the roof of a nearby house
as if it were made of wrapping paper.
Then it toppled a lorry on to its side,
leaving only the wipers
waving frantically for help.

But today the weather,
sent fingers of light
to creep into my bedroom
and offer a warming hand.
It seemed to be an apology
for yesterday's stormy temper.

Ask the children the following questions about the poem:
● What did they think was the most interesting part of the poem?
● Did the poem make them think of other storms?
● What did it mean by 'my bedroom window shivering on the wall'? How else could you say this?
● How can the cold lick your face? Does it make sense to liken the storm to an animal or creature?
● The last verse compares the storm to someone having lost his temper. Can they compare the storm to something else such as a battle, a loud musical party or perhaps a play or story being performed in the skies?

Transport

Age range
Seven to eleven.

What to do

Read the rap poem 'Stuck here forever' to the children. They will probably enjoy joining in on the refrain and you can introduce actions. In fact the children will learn the poem very quickly. Follow the reading with a discussion of the children's own experiences of being stuck in traffic jams. Other areas to explore might be:
● What is their favourite form of transport?
● Is there any type of major transport they haven't yet experienced?
● What do they do to pass the time when they are caught in a traffic jam or travelling long distances?
● Can they think of descriptions for various forms of transport such as sleek limousines, crowded buses, lumbering lorries and so on?

Stuck here forever!

1st gear,
          2nd gear,
                    3rd gear – NEVER,
are we to be stuck in this traffic jam FOREVER!

With,
cars slowing and traffic growing,
bumpers nudging, hardly budging.
Stop – start, stop – start, NO OVERTAKING!
Stop – start, stop – start, CONTINUAL BRAKING!

1st gear,
          2nd gear,
                    3rd gear – NEVER,
are we to be stuck in this traffic jam FOREVER!

With,
babies crying and mothers sighing,
drivers glaring and horns blaring.
HONK! HONK! HONK! PEEP! PEEP! PEEP!
CARS, CARS, CARS like SHEEP, SHEEP, SHEEP!

1st gear,
       2nd gear,
             3rd gear – NEVER,
are we to be stuck in this traffic jam FOREVER!

Engines turning and fumes burning,
petrol oxidising and pollution rising.
SMOKE! SMOKE! SMOKE!
CHOKE! CHOKE! CHOKE!
A solution to pollution – a masterstroke!

1st hour,
       2nd hour,
             3rd hour's gone,
I'LL BE ANOTHER YEAR OLDER BEFORE WE MOVE ON!

  Ask the children to write a transport poem. This could be done from many points of view, but you might like to follow the example of the poem and get them to write a poem that emphasises movement. This can be achieved through description or, as in the example of the poem, through rhythm and rhyme.

My window

Age range
Seven to eleven.

What to do
Ask the children to find a window with an interesting view either inside the school or at home and to take notes about what they see. You may need to explain to them about horizons, foreground, double glazing, different types of window, levels in houses and so on.
  Once they have done this read them 'From my window'.

From my window

From my window I see
the lonely tree at the bottom of our garden
waving to catch my attention.
'Come and look, come and look',
its long fingers seem to be saying.

But I'm drawn upwards
off towards black lumps of cloud
that swagger into view
as if they are chasing trouble.
'Move over sun, your time's up',
they appear to announce
as daylight suffers a short power loss.

Down on the streets cars are playing
'Now you see me, now you don't,'
behind neighbouring houses,
while in the distant skyline
a train rushes along chattering,
'Mustn't be late, mustn't be late!'

Discuss the poem with the children:
● What sort of tree did the poet see?
● What colour were the clouds?

● What game were the cars playing?
● What did the train appear to be saying?
● What else do they think the poet might have seen from her window?

Ask the children to write their own 'Through the window' poems. The following questions may help them.
● Where is their window?
● Is the window on an upper or lower level?
● What can they see from their window in the foreground and in the distance?
● How does the view alter during the day?
● What happens when darkness falls?
● If they open their window what difference does this make?

The children can, if you wish, design or draw their own windows to decorate their poems. They can make little curtains to open and close over their window poems.

Old age

Age range
Eight to eleven.

What to do
It helps with this idea if the children are given prior notice so they can observe their subject in detail. They may choose a grandparent or someone living in their street but it should be an elderly person that they know or can observe in detail. They need to be directed to look at how the elderly person moves, what he wears, his hands and face as well as how he sounds. They might be able to see inside his home and reflect on his life-style. The children, in some cases, may have noticed the changes in their subject in the years they have known them.

'My granddad' should hopefully help the children to start to think of special habits or mannerisms that their elderly person may have and the jokes or sayings that they use.

My granddad

My granddad is as round shouldered as a question mark
and is led about all day by his walking stick.
With teeth that aren't real,
hidden behind a moustache that is,
while his memories simmer warmly
inside his crinkled paper bag of a face.

My granddad,
old and worn on the outside,
sparky and fresh on the in.
For he often,
shakes my hand with fifty pence pieces,
makes sweets pop out from behind his ears,
smokes all day like a train
then laughs like one as well.
Plays jokes on my mother
as he tries to freshen her face with a smile
and then tells me stories that electrify my brain.

But best of all,
when my dad loses his temper,
Grandpa just tells him
TO SIT DOWN AND BEHAVE HIMSELF.

Good old grandpa!

Ask the children to write their own poems on old age.

Playgrounds

Age range
Eight to eleven.

What to do

An interesting and possibly contentious area of the
school to write about is the playground. The poem 'Our
side of the playground' can be used to set a discussion
in motion. Do they think that the comments are fair? If
not, then how is their own behaviour different? Whether
you wish to get the children to write from their own sex's
point of view or simply write generally about their
playground will be up to how you direct the class.

Our side of the playground!

Being the teacher
I asked the question,
'Which side of the playground is most fun?'
And the answers fired out quickly, one by one.

The girls said,
'We don't pretend to be cars
and end up covered in scars.
We don't scream and charge
or push around and barge.
We don't bruise and bump
then walk off with the hump.
We don't chase a ball all day,
out of breath and nothing to say.
And we don't thud around with mud around.
No, girls like to be sensible and quiet
not the cause of a raging riot!'

The boys said,
'We don't play Dads and Mums
and stand sucking thumbs.
We don't play kiss chases
then admire our spotty faces.
We don't imitate a pop star
then dress up all bizarre.
We don't spend all day talking
like parrots when they're squawking.
And we don't take up with make-up.
No, boys want to compete with each other
not practise at being mother.'

So the result was that neither side was covered in
glory.
But then again there's always two sides to every story!

The following ideas should be discussed in direct response to the poem and then from a general viewpoint.
● Which points in the poem do they agree or disagree with?
● Do they think the poem is fair to both sides or does it favour one in particular?
● What did the poet mean by saying 'there's always two sides to every story'? Was this a good way to finish the poem?
● Are there any other points that might have been mentioned?

Having discussed the poem the children can write their own poem about the playground. They can use the following questions to help them if you wish.
● How do you feel when you go out to play?
● Describe the playground. Does it remind you of anything, for example, a zoo, a fairground, a circus?
● Where do you normally play?
● Are there quiet areas in your playground?
● Think of words to describe children in the playground – charging, yelling, sprinting.
● If the playground was a person what would it be thinking?
● How would you improve your playground?
● How do you feel when you come in from the playground?

Catch a creature!

Age range
Eight to eleven.

What to do
Read to the children the poem 'Instructions for catching the spider'.

Instructions for catching the spider

Slip it between an upturned cup
Or tumbler and a postcard
Carefully slid in under it, remembering
That just because it doesn't buzz
You can't assume
It likes the darkness.

Walk to the door
Or nearest window if it opens easily,
Slide back the postcard, let
The light in, gently tip the cup
Or tumbler, wait
Until the spider's ready.

Watch it hang a moment
In a web of air
As if somehow attached to it
before it drifts down, landing
Right-way-up because its legs are everywhere,
And scampers off across the garden.

John Mole

Once you have read the poem the children will slowly begin to mention other creatures they would consider capturing and also letting go. This list can start off with small creatures and may grow in size and imagination to include such things as flies, mice, birds, lions, rhinoceroses, unicorns and so on. Discuss with the children the various forms of catching a particular creature the children usually come up with some ingenious ideas. Ask them to write their own poems about how to catch a creature of their choice.

Imagination

Age range
Nine to eleven.

What to do
A simple way to encourage children to stretch their imagination is by asking them to imagine whatever they would like to be and then explain what they would do. Read them the following poem to help explain the idea.

If

If I were a storm,
I'd blacken the sky
then scar it with flashes of lightning.
I'd shake everybody's bedroom windows,
saturate everything I could find
and then thunder with laughter!

Once the children have grasped the idea they will be able to come up with plenty of topics to write about themselves, but for those who might struggle you could suggest that they begin with a clock, a pen, snow, the sun, the sea, a school, a book or a television set.

Music and song

Age range
Nine to eleven.

What to do
Ask the children to bring to school some tapes of their favourite pop songs. Play these songs and let the children choose four or five favourites. Give each group a song and ask them to listen to them and write out the lyrics.

Ask the children to consider the following questions:
● What is the title of the song?
● What is the song all about?
● Which are the parts of the lyrics they enjoy most – the rhyme or a particular repeated refrain?
● Would they alter the lyrics or title?
  Bring all the groups together and let the children discuss as a class what they feel makes a good pop song and how important the lyrics are.

Follow-up
Ask the children to write their own pop songs and put them to music. Afterwards they could vote to find out the most popular song.

The one-upmanship poem

Age range
Nine to eleven.

What to do
A novel activity which often appeals to older children is one involving words with numbers and also words with number sounding syllables in them such as won – one and for/tun/ate – four/tun/eight. Ask the children to write out sentences, or indeed short poems, with the number words and the number syllables underlined.

The next step is to play one-upmanship. Here the children should read their pieces out loud and as they do so to add one to each number word or number syllable, for example:

Once upon a time
there lived a fortunate boy.
would become:
Twice upon a time
there live a fivetunnine boy.

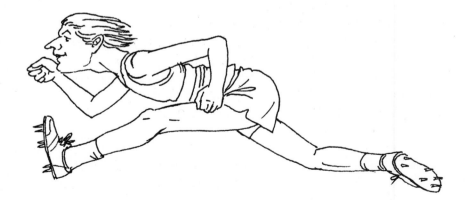

You can also read the following poem to the children and let them play one-upmanship.

The fortunate boy

Once upon a time
there lived a fortunate boy
called Tudor Forsyth
who was wonderfully good at sport.
At the school sports he won
the three-legged race,
the running by one fifth of a second
and the wheelbarrow race almost on all fours.
He was in seventh heaven
when in the tennis competition.
One by one he overcame all his opponents
to reach the final.
However, before the game
he did become rather tense
and started talking nineteen to the dozen.
Eventually the match began at four o'clock
and was rather one-sided.
Even though Tudor played with a sore forefinger
he dominated with his formidable double-handed backhand
and the game was soon won.
After his winning day
Tudor returned home for forty winks.
Unfortunately he never repeated his performance again
For due to injury his days as a successful sportsman were numbered!

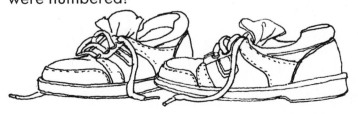

Reproducible material

Rhyming word sheet, see pages 19 and 26

back	pram	sand	care	place	plate	whee	leak	cheap
pack	ram	stand	chair	race	rate	—	leek	cheep
rack	scram	—	dare	space	skate	each	peek	creep
sack	slam	bang	fair	—	slate	beach	sneak	heap
slack	—	clang	fare	brass	wait	beech	speak	keep
snack	brain	rang	glare	class	—	peach	squeak	leap
stack	chain	sang	hair	gas	at	reach	weak	peep
tack	crane	sprang	hare	glass	bat	speech	—	sheep
whack	drain	—	pair	grass	brat	teach	check	sleep
—	again	bank	rare	lass	cat	—	deck	steep
gale	lane	blank	scare	mass	chat	bead	fleck	weep
jail	pain	crank	spare	pass	fat	bleed	neck	—
mail	plane	drank	square	—	flat	deed	peck	ear
male	rain	plank	stair	crash	hat	feed	speck	beer
nail	Spain	rank	stare	dash	mat	greed	wreck	cheer
pail	sprain	—	wear	flash	pat	lead	—	clear
rail	train	cap	where	lash	rat	need	deal	dear
sail	—	chap	—	rash	sat	read	feel	deer
scale	can	clap	art	smash	scat	seed	heal	fear
tail	fan	flap	cart	splash	that	speed	heel	hear
whale	began	gap	chart	—	—	weed	meal	near
—	man	lap	dart	blast	bee	—	kneel	rear
aim	pan	map	heart	cast	flea	bed	peal	spear
blame	plan	nap	part	fast	free	bread	peel	tear
came	ran	rap	smart	last	he	dead	seal	year
fame	span	wrap	start	mast	key	fed	squeal	—
game	tan	scrap	tart	past	knee	head	steal	eat
lame	than	slap	—	vast	me	led	—	beat
name	van	snap	base	—	quay	lead	bell	cheat
same	—	strap	brace	ate	pea	read	fell	feat
tame	and	tap	case	eight	sea	red	sell	feet
—	band	trap	chase	crate	see	said	shell	meat
gram	brand	—	face	date	she	tread	smell	meet
ham	grand	air	grace	hate	tea	—	tell	street
jam	hand	bare	lace	late	tree	beak	well	sweet
lamb	land	bear	pace	mate	we	creak	—	treat

Rhyming word sheet, see pages 19 and 26

bet	brick	mink	tight	dock	moan	sore	
get	chick	pink	write	flock	phone	snore	
forget	click	rink	—	frock	shown	store	
jet	flick	shrink	blow	knock	stone	tore	
let	kick	sink	flow	loch	thrown	your	glue
met	lick	stink	glow	lock	—	—	grew
net	pick	think	go	rock	book	boat	shoe
pet	quick	wink	grow	shock	brook	coat	stew
set	sick	—	low	sock	cook	float	two
sweat	stick	chip	no	stock	crook	goat	who
wet	thick	clip	know	—	hook	note	—
—	—	drip	row	ox	look	wrote	bug
breeze	ill	flip	so	box	rook	throat	hug
cheese	chill	grip	slow	fox	shook	—	lug
freeze	kill	hip	snow	locks	took	bow	jug
knees	mill	lip	throw	socks	—	cow	plug
peas	skill	nip	toe	—	chop	how	rug
please	spill	rip	tow	all	crop	allow	snug
seize	still	ship	—	ball	drop	row	thug
tease	will	snip	dog	call	flop	wow	—
wheeze	—	tip	flog	fall	hop	—	cool
—	bring	trip	fog	shawl	mop	brown	fool
eye	fling	whip	frog	stall	pop	clown	rule
buy	king	—	hog	tall	shop	crown	school
cry	ring	bright	jog	—	swap	down	tool
die	sing	fight	log	own	top	drown	—
dry	spring	flight	—	blown	—	frown	bloom
fly	sting	fright	oil	bone	oar	gown	broom
fry	string	height	boil	cone	door	noun	gloom
my	swing	kite	coil	flown	floor	town	room
pie	thing	light	foil	groan	four	—	tomb
shy	—	might	soil	grown	more	blue	zoom
sky	ink	night	spoil	known	pour	clue	
sly	blink	quite	toil	loan	roar	crew	
why	chink	right	—	lone	shore	do	
—	drink	sight	clock	alone	soar	flew	

Nonsense worksheet, see page 30

Read the sentences below and then have fun mixing them up e.g. The itchy witch cooked a nappy.

The	evil	witch	cooked	a	tomato
The	orange	monkey	climbed	a	tree
The	angry	giant	squeezed	a	banana
The	itchy	baby	grabbed	a	nappy
The	excited	popstar	smashed	a	piano

Now try and write your own sentences in the grid below.

When you have finished writing and reading your sentences why not exchange your sheet with someone in your class?

The rhyming wheel, see pages 22, 23, 48 and 60

Cut out both wheels and centre the smaller wheel on top of the bigger one.
Now place a paper fastener through the middle.

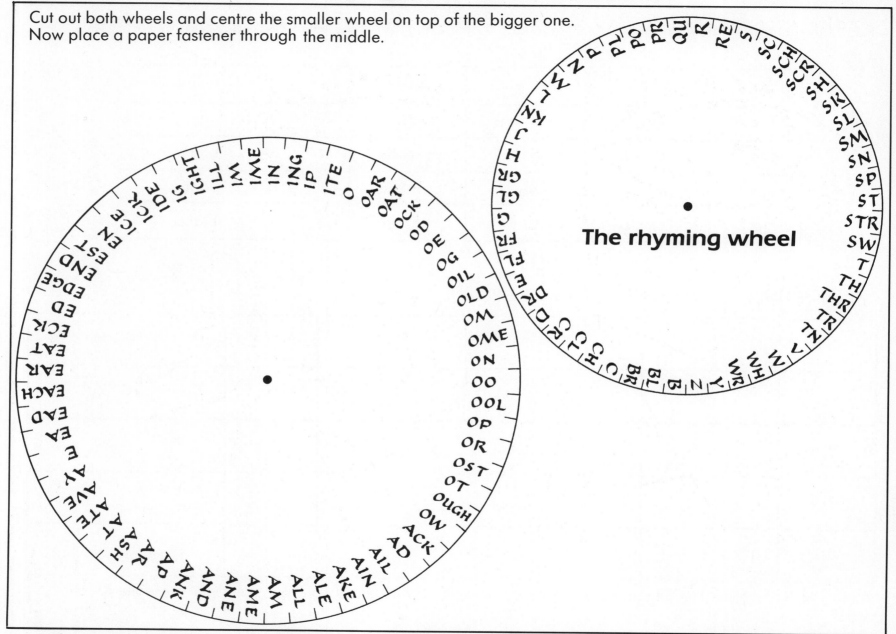

The rhyming wheel

Shapes for writing, see page 52

Have fun writing round the following shapes. Remember it does not have to rhyme!

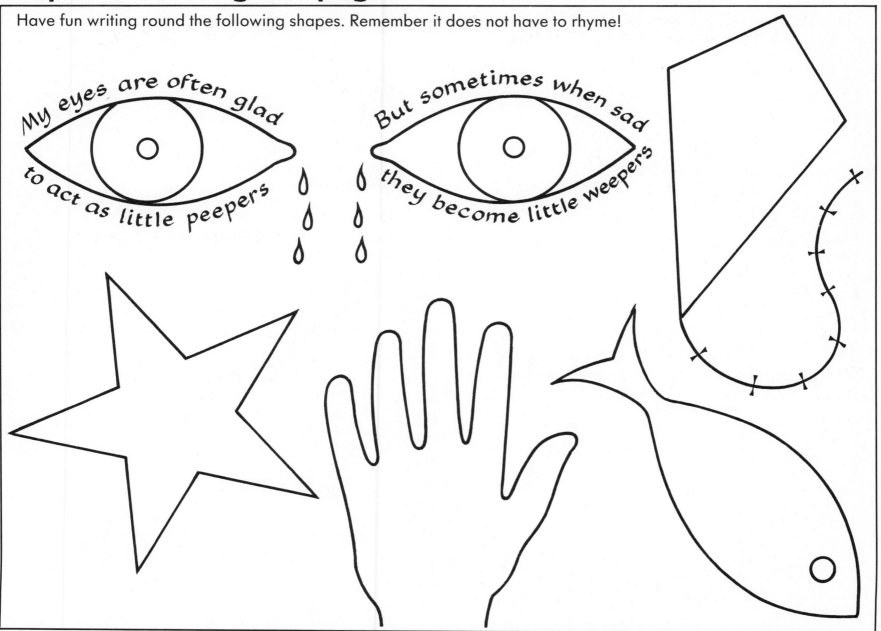

My eyes are often glad to act as little peepers

But sometimes when sad they become little weepers

Styles and forms of poetry, see page 70

When you are familiar with the different forms decorate these pages and keep them for reference.

Personification

The early morning

The early morning
exhales a cool breath
over the lifeless, languid trees.
Gradually,
they stretch themselves awake
and rhythmically begin
exercising their taunt, brown limbs.

Limerick

A teacher from Harrow
There was a young teacher from Harrow
Whose nose was too long and too narrow.
It gave so much trouble
That he bent it double
And wheeled it round school in a barrow.

Cinquain

Space,
Mysterious, alien,
Absorbing, fascinating, challenging,
Stretching out into infinity,
Universal.

Diamante

City
busy, noisy
bustling, sprawling, polluting
streets, roads, ——— fields, lanes
farming, flowering, blossoming
scenic, tranquil
Countryside

Collective

Yesterday I noticed,
a buzz of bees,
a chapter of books,
a cuddle of coats,
a team of footballs,
a bag of belly buttons,
a roof of houses,
a scribble of pens
and an exhaust of cars.

They were all cool, calm and collected!

Couplet

The early morning sun;
An orange balloon waiting to be popped.

Haiku

Autumn trees

Proudly they stand;
upturned paint brushes
daubed in rustic hues.

Nonsense

I said my pyjamas

I said my pyjamas,
I put on my prayers,
I went up my slippers,
I took off my stairs,
I switch off the bed,
I jumped in the light,
The reason for this is
You kissed me goodnight.

Definition

What's night?

A dark ceiling,
a blackboard of sky,
a light-taker,
a shadow-maker,
an announcement of sleep,
a nightmare and dream time.

That's sleep!

Metaphoric

Bombers!

Engines buzz,
wings flap,
as yellow aerodynamic bodies
hit the air.
Black insignia,
an omen to all
of a possible sting in the tail.
Venom tipped missiles
armed for launching.

Sensible work, see page 84

Fill in the sheet with the help of a thesaurus and then keep it for future reference.

Taste Words	Touch Words	Sound Words
1. oily	1. tickle	1, bang
2. bitter	2. stroke	2. squeak
3.	3.	3.
4.	4.	4.
5.	5.	5.
6.	6.	6.
7.	7.	7.
8.	8.	8.
9.	9.	9.
10.	10.	10.

Smell Words	Colour Words	Movement Words
1. delicious	1. brilliant	1. swift
2. stale	2. dull	2. graceful
3.	3.	3.
4.	4.	4.
5.	5.	5.
6.	6.	6.
7.	7.	7.
8.	8.	8.
9.	9.	9.
10.	10.	10.

On the back of this sheet write down ten shape words, e.g. wide, ten age words, e.g. old, and ten size words e.g. tiny.

Rhyming wordsearches

Can you find the following
'ar' words
in the wordsearch?

1. car
2. jar
3. star
4. far
5. par
6. bar
7. tar
8. scar

Can you now make
up your own
rhyming wordsearch?

1.
2.
3.
4.
5.
6.
7.
8.

AR

D	J	A	R	S	C	A	R
T	A	B	E	B	F	A	T
P	D	S	T	A	R	C	F
O	F	A	L	F	A	R	J
C	A	R	O	R	A	M	T
T	S	W	B	A	R	N	O
P	C	T	A	R	E	U	V
F	D	A	B	A	P	A	R

Poetry wordsearches

1. Find the following words inside the wordsearch.

1. verse
2. couplets
3. poet
4. limerick
5. haiku
6. rhymes
7. metre
8. prose
9. senses
10. calligram
11. descriptions
12. riddles

2. Now hide the following words in the same way and then get someone to find them!

1. rhythm
2. shape
3. nonsense
4. patterns
5. syllables
6. metaphors
7. imagery
8. similes
9. jokes
10. word play
11. alliteration
12. traditional

C	E	S	C	A	L	S	P	D	S	V	L
D	V	E	R	S	E	I	R	B	N	E	M
R	S	N	A	N	E	G	O	M	O	R	A
I	C	P	S	S	K	R	U	E	I	S	R
D	P	E	O	U	C	K	E	T	T	A	G
D	S	R	B	K	I	T	R	R	P	M	I
L	P	H	Y	A	R	R	M	E	I	R	L
E	L	R	H	N	E	H	E	E	R	H	L
S	I	T	W	A	M	Y	T	A	C	Y	A
H	P	E	T	V	I	M	P	R	S	T	C
T	C	O	U	P	L	E	T	S	E	O	W
W	H	P	U	D	D	S	M	R	D	L	S

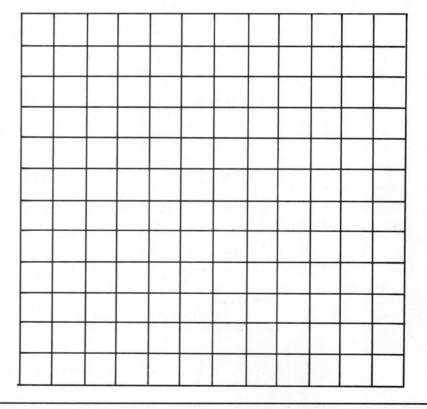

Jean Bean and Blair Dare

There are two creatures hidden in the picture below. They are called Jean Bean and Blair Dare. To find them you have to colour in the shapes which contain words that rhyme with their names. There are eight words for each creature. Watch out! The words may not be spelled in the same way but still sound the same.

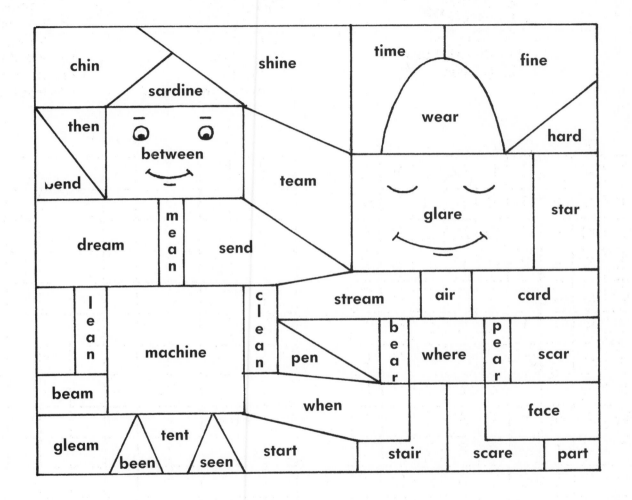

Now using the rhyming words you found try and make up a sentence about each creature using as many of those words as you can, e.g., Jean Bean has been seen on a green, mean machine which wasn't clean!

Poetry book record

Fill in this sheet when you have finished reading a poetry book.

Date	Book	Poet/ compiler	Favourite poem	Book score	How to score your poetry books	
					Catastrophe	0
					Awful	1
					No, not really	2
					You have to be deperate	3
					Only just	4
					U may find it satisfactory	5
					Just about getting there	6
					U should enjoy it	7
					Definitely	8
					Great	9
					Excellent – read it now!	10
					?	

Resources

Recommended books

Anthologies

Is a Caterpillar Ticklish? collected by Adrian Rumble (1989, Young Puffin Books).
A fine collection of poems for top infants and lower juniors.
Junior Poetry Anthology: The First Lick of the Lolly (1986), *Marbles in my Pocket* (1986), *Go and Open the Door* (1987), *The Unicorn and the Lions* (1987), compiled by Moira Andrew (Thomas Nelson).
Another splendid series of anthologies for the full primary range.
The Kingfisher Book of Children's Poetry, by Michael Rosen (1985, Kingfisher).
A book that offers a real potpourri of poetic enjoyment. More for the top junior age range.
The Last Rabbit (1990) and *Dove on the Roof* (1992), edited by Jennifer Curry (Mammoth).
Two first class anthologies. The former is about conservation and the latter deals with peace.
Madtail, Miniwhale and Other Shape Poems, compiled by Wes Magee (1989, Puffin Books).
If you are looking for a book on shape poems then this is for you.
Scholastic Collections: Early Years Poems and Rhymes, compiled by Jill Bennett (1993, Scholastic).
A rich collection of over 400 poems for the early years. The book has been compiled under a varied selection of headings with many poems especially written for the book.
Scholastic Collections: Poetry, compiled by Wes Magee (1992, Scholastic).
A bumper book of contemporary and traditional poetry. A must for any school.
This Little Puffin: finger play and nursery games, compiled by Elizabeth Matterson (1991, Puffin Books).
Another classic in its own right full of finger plays and nursery games to stimulate and interest the very young.
Tiny Tim: Verses for children, compiled by Jill Bennett (1984, Armada Books). Still as popular as ever with young and older children alike.

Twinkle Twinkle Chocolate Bar, compiled by John Foster (1992, Oxford University Press).
An excellent selection of rhymes for the very young with delightful illustrations.
A Very First (1979), *Second* (1981), *Third* (1982), *Fourth* (1983), *Fifth* (1986) *Poetry Book* plus the *Another: First* (1988), *Second* (1988), *Third* (1988), *Fourth* (1989), *Fifth* (1989) *Poetry Book*, compiled by John Foster (Oxford University Press).
This series covers the full primary range and sets a high standard as regards the choice of material and the excellent use of illustrations.
The Walker Book of Poetry for Children, compiled by Jack Prelutsky (1984, Walker).
Another jumbo anthology but well worth the money. It has a strong American flavour and is brimming with invaluable poems to suit all moods and situations.
What on Earth . . .? Poems with a conservation theme, edited by Judith Nicholls (1989, Faber).
Another fine collection of conservation poems.
A Year Full of Poems, compiled by Michael Harrison and Christopher Stuart-Clark (1991, Oxford University Press).
As with the previous book it contains poems discussing and reflecting the months and seasons. It sets just as high a standard and has some beautiful illustrations.
You Just Can't Win, compiled by Brian Moses (1991, Blackie).
A lively and hugely enjoyable anthology that manages to be both humorous and thoughtful in dealing with family life.

Single collections

All Together Now! (1990) and *Smile Please!* (1989), by Tony Bradman (Puffin Books).
Mainly rhyming poems that look at various aspects of young children's lives in generally a light, humorous fashion.
Bears Don't Like Bananas, by John Rice (1991, Simon and Schuster Young Books).
Splendid poems generally about animals and nature.
The Butterfly Jar, by Jeff Moss (1991, Piper).
Jeff Moss was the head writer for Sesame Street. Again originality and nonsense reigns supreme!
Catching the Spider (1990) and *The Conjuror's Rabbit* (1992), by John Mole (Blackie).
Poems to make you reflect, consider and smile.
The Dragon on the Wall (1989), *The Poem Box* (1991), *The Squirrel in Town* (1988), by Stanley Cook (Blackie).
If you are looking for thoughtful poems for the young then look no further – simply the best!
I Din' Do Nuttin' and Other Poems (1983, Magnet) *Say it Again Granny: Twenty poems from Caribbean proverbs* (1986, Little Mammoth), by John Agard.
Lively and at times thoughtful collections for the young by a Guyanese poet.
Jelly Belly, by Dennis Lee (1987, Picturemac)
A delightful collection of modern rhymes by a Canadian poet.
A Light in the Attic (1982) and *Where the Sidewalk Ends* (1984), by Shel Silverstein (Jonathan Cape).
A master at original, nonsense poetry. Ideal for those who like to smile while having their imaginations stretched!
Morning Break and other poems, by Wes Magee (1989, Cambridge University Press).
As a former head teacher Wes Magee knows how to hit the spot with this diverse collection.
Please Mrs Butler, by Allan Ahlberg (1984, Penguin).
An extremely popular collection of school verse.
Rabbiting On, by Kit Wright (1978, Armada Books).
A collection of witty, joyful poems not to be missed.
Salford Road and other poems (1979) and *Song of the City* (1985), by Gareth Owen (Lion).
Poems that taste strongly of childhood and growing up. You should enjoy the flavour. The book is more for top juniors.
Sky in the Pie (1984, Puffin Books), *Pillow Talk* (1990, Viking) and *You Tell me* written by Michael Rosen (1979, Puffin Books), by Roger McGough.
Plenty of word play, witty thoughts and poems to enjoy.
Songs For my Dog and Other People (out of print, 1980) and *Wry Rhymes for Troublesome Times* (1985), by Max Fatchen (Puffin Books).
Imaginative nonsense seen through the eyes of an Australian poet. Both great fun and full of clever rhymes.
The Word Party (1986, Lutterworth Press) and *Whispers from a Wardrobe* (1987, Lutterworth Press), by Richard Edwards.
Original and entertaining poetry.
You Can't Catch Me (1981, Picture Puffin), *Don't Put Mustard in the Custard* (1987, Picture Lion), *Quick Let's Get Out of Here* (1983, Puffin Books) and *The Hypnotiser* (1991, Young Lions), by Michael Rosen.
Michael Rosen has the ability to make the ordinary suddenly interesting and amusing. Some extremely funny story poems. The children love them!

Joke books

The Crack-a-Joke Book, edited by Kaye Webb (out of print, 1978, Puffin Books). Jokes chosen by children for children. Great fun if you can find a copy.
The Ha Ha Bonk Book, by Janet and Allan Ahlberg (1982, Young Puffin Books). Still the best of its kind, supplying jokes that young children can enjoy and understand.

Books for teaching poetry

Catapults and Kingfishers: Teaching poetry in primary schools, by Pie Corbett and Brian Moses (1986, Oxford University Press).
An excellent resource as regards the teaching of poetry in primary schools. A book that can be dipped into or followed progressively. It offers a wide selection of ideas for stimulating children with an introduction which clearly and succinctly explains how to set about teaching poetry.

Catching the Light, by Brian Moses (1992, World Wide Fund).
A book that helps teachers to cover very important environmental issues with 5–8 year olds. Areas such as neighbourhood, towns, cities, seashore, countryside, waste and recycling are presented in an interesting fashion with lots of stimulating poetry activities.
Does It Have To Rhyme? by Sandy Brownjohn (1980, Hodder and Stoughton).
Definitely for top juniors, especially if using the included poems as examples but still full of good ideas and exercises for encouraging children to write poetry.
The Essential Guide to Poetry by David Orme (1992, Folens).
An excellent well-structured guide to the teaching of poetry in the classroom.
Inspirations for Poetry, by Helen Hadley (1992, Scholastic).
You'll never run short of ideas with this book around. A splendid bumper book that covers many aspects of teaching poetry.
Language in Colour: Themes for infants and lower juniors with poetry as the starting point, by Moira Andrew (1989, Belair).
A well produced book with the ideas and poems laid out in a clear, succinct fashion. It is aimed at top infants and lower juniors covering fourteen topics dealing with the gardens, water and weather. The teaching points and their progression are excellent, reflecting the experience and expertise of Moira Andrew.
Start-Write, edited by Morag Styles (1986, EARO – now Education IT, The Resource Centre, Back Hill, Ely, Cambridgeshire CB7 4DA).
An interesting book full of practical ideas on how to start children writing poetry. There are many contributions by practising teachers and fine examples of children's work.

Miscellaneous

Resource items
BBC Sounds effects tapes available from most high street record shops.
The New Where's That Poem? by Helen Morris (1992, Simon and Schuster).
Children's poems organised under subject headings. So if you are looking for a particular poem or type of poem this book would be a great help.
The Oxford Children's Thesaurus and *The Oxford Study Thesaurus* compiled by A. Spooner (Oxford University Press).

These books are well organised and generally easy to use. For words with multiple meanings these books number and give examples of how the word can be used in different situations.
Poetry 0–16, compiled by Morag Styles and Pat Triggs (1988, Books for Keeps).
A first-class resource and for those who are hooked on poetry this is a must.

Poetry competitions
The Roald Dahl Foundation Poetry Competition – Cadbury's have withdrawn their sponsorship from the National Exhibition of Children's Art but thankfully The Roald Dahl Foundation have stepped in. A new competition is to be announced and the details to be sent out to schools during the spring of 1993.
W.H. Smith Young Writers' Competition – Held every year between October and February. The winners are usually announced in February.
Public Relations
W.H. Smith Group plc.
Strand House
7 Holbein Place
London SW1W 8NR

The Poetry Society
The Poetry Society promotes poetry and poets in education. It also administers the W.H. Smith 'Poets in School' scheme, produces the B.P. Teachers' Poetry Resource Files and has recently merged with the Schools' Poetry Association which now offers an excellent termly journal entitled *School Poetry Review* plus a variety of other services.
For details of the Poetry Society write to:
Sally Bacon, Education Officer, The Poetry Society, 22 Betterton Street, London WC2H 9BU (Please enclose a s.a.e.)

Copyright acknowledgements